Wicked OTTAWA COUNTY MICHIGAN

Wicked OTTAWA COUNTY MICHIGAN

AMBERROSE HAMMOND

THE History PRESS

Published by The History Press
Charleston, SC 29403
www.historypress.net

First published 2011

Manufactured in the United States

ISBN 978.1.60949.174.1

Hammond, Amberrose.
Wicked Ottawa County, Michigan / Amberrose Hammond.
p. cm.
Includes bibliographical references.
ISBN 978-1-60949-174-1
1. Crime--Michigan--Ottawa County--History--Anecdotes. 2. Murder--Michigan--Ottawa County--History--Anecdotes. 3. Violence--Michigan--Ottawa County--History--Anecdotes. 4. Corruption--Michigan--Ottawa County--History--Anecdotes. 5. Ottawa County (Mich.)--History--Anecdotes. 6. Ottawa County (Mich.)--Biography--Anecdotes. 7. Ottawa County (Mich.)--Social conditions--Anecdotes. 8. Ottawa County (Mich.)--Moral conditions--Anecdotes. I. Title.
HV6795.O88H36 2011
364.109774'15--dc23
2011032574

Notice: The information in this book is true and complete to the best of our knowledge. It is offered without guarantee on the part of the author or The History Press. The author and The History Press disclaim all liability in connection with the use of this book.

This book is dedicated to Jeanette Weiden for her amazing detective skills.
(Told you I'd do it.)

Contents

Acknowledgements

If it wasn't for my Loutit District Library, I would never have been able to write this book. Please continue to support your public libraries, as they are so very important to a community. I'd like to thank the members of the Dusty Dozens who have welcomed me into their group and inspired me to love our local and state history even more. You are an amazing bunch of historians and people! Bob Beaton, for the endless work he has done with indexing old stories on Sandhill City. The Carl Bajema Collection, for its inspiration and story leads. Mike Faulkner, for supplying information and enthusiasm in the George Seelman story. It's always awesome to meet someone actually connected to a story I write. Ruth Horton, for her genealogy on the Shield family. Herrick District Library, for its assistance on some Holland area history. The History Press, for giving me the opportunity to write this book and my first book, *Ghosts & Legends of Michigan's West Coast*. You have inspired awesome possibilities in me. My family, grandparents and mother, who are always excited about what crazy project I'm doing next. Tom Maat, for just being an awesome partner in crime in whatever I do. Julie Williams, for always listening—again! And to all of the crazy lives that were lived in the past that made this book possible.

Introduction

Welcome to the wilds of west Michigan! Our history in sleepy, picturesque Ottawa County might seem pretty tame to its residents and visitors. We have pastel dunes, miles of beautiful Lake Michigan coastline and busy little tourist towns bursting with people in the summer months. But buried in those shifting sand dunes are fascinating, shocking, witty and sometimes gruesome stories. Our ancestors dealt with their share of murder and mayhem, just like we do today.

My interest in this project took root when I started writing my first book for The History Press, *Ghosts & Legends of Michigan's West Coast*. As I collected tales about haunted locations and the history behind them, I uncovered stories of murders, bank robberies and other dastardly deeds. I saved them all out of morbid interest, and when it came around to thinking of another project to work on, the idea of putting these tales came together in the form of this book. Writing these stories was like piecing an eggshell back together sometimes. There were so many details and nuances that it made my head spin at times.

I was even motivated to write this by my own family history—a little bootlegging on the side, as well as other little "wicked" things. My great-great-grandma Volovlek came from Yugoslavia to the United States in the early 1900s. Great-great-grandma Volovlek was quite the legend in our family history. She was a midwife who delivered a lot of children in her day around Grand Haven, even her own grandchildren. She first migrated to Wisconsin when she came to the States and owned a boardinghouse. She

An early Ottawa County Atlas. *Courtesy of Loutit District Library.*

was a bigger lady who always wore a long dress and an apron, so everyone was in shock when one night she served the boarders dinner at the house, went upstairs and came downstairs with a baby in her arms. The baby was hers, and no one even knew she had been pregnant. She actually delivered her own child.

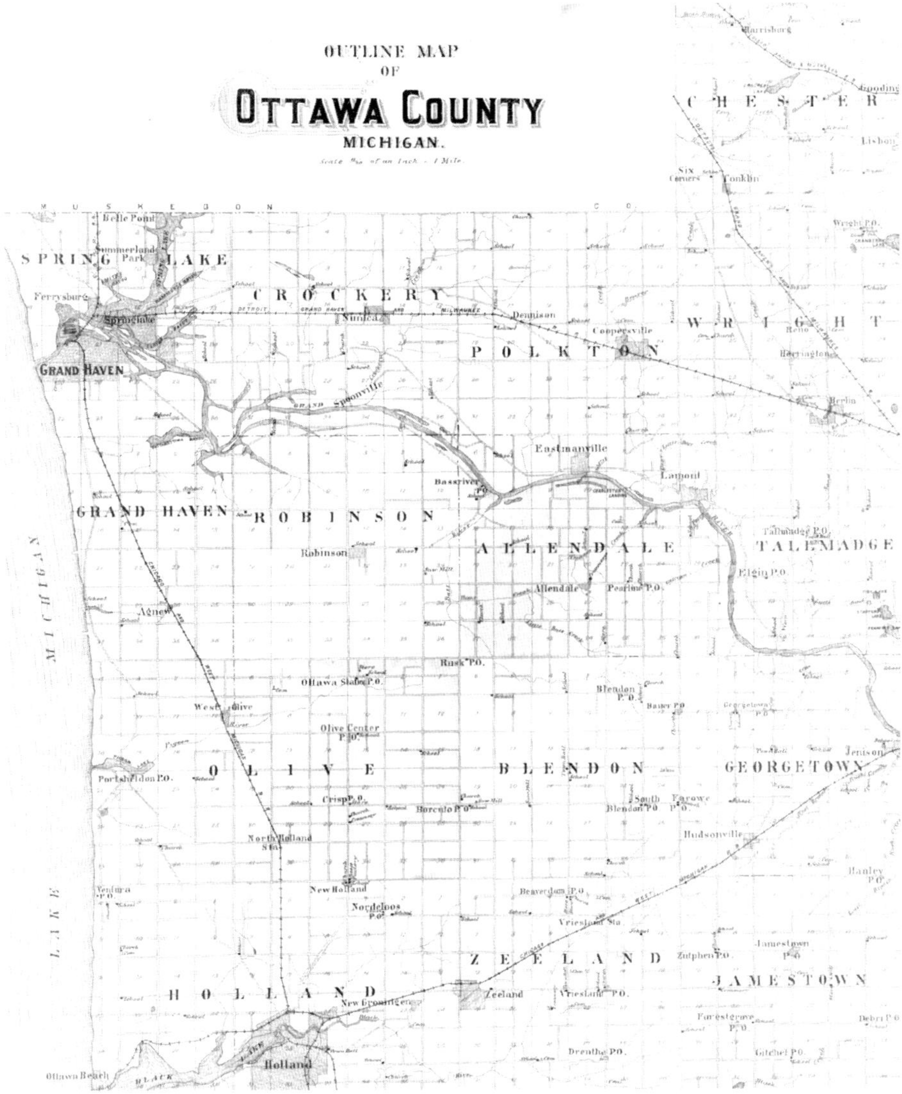

An early plat map of Ottawa County. *Courtesy of Loutit District Library.*

She and her husband owned a farm off M45 in Robinson Township with chickens, cows, pigs, horses, fruit trees, grapevines and plenty of homemade booze to supply some of the notables around Grand Haven during the Prohibition era. It was always said that she even spent a night in jail for her illegal sales. And the stories don't stop there. My great-grandma and grandpa Resner made their own share of wine and beer as well. We still have the large wooden wine casks they once used in the winemaking process.

BLOOD SAUSAGE

When my grandma and her sister were little girls, it was a big event when great-great-grandma Volovlek was slaughtering the pigs and getting the smokehouse ready for the meat to hang. The family always made a dish called blood sausage, which by all means does not sound too tempting. But on Sundays, after the kids had to fast for twelve hours before taking communion at the local Catholic church, the sausage would be put into the oven and ready to eat when everyone came home from church. The smell of the cooked sausage filled the house, and everyone's mouths watered as they entered the kitchen. It was always something to look forward to.

So when my young grandma and her sister went to great-great-grandma Volovlek's farm for a pig slaughter, they weren't prepared to find out exactly how blood sausage got its name. They stood there in their pretty dresses and watched as Uncle Joe took an axe to a pig's neck. Blood started spraying everywhere and on Uncle Joe as the pig whipped its body around, reacting to the pain. As the blood poured out of the pig's neck, great-great-grandma Volovlek grabbed on to the pig, got a bucket and started to collect the blood spilling out, telling my grandma's sister to grab a cake pan, too, and try to collect as much blood as possible. My grandma's sister can still remember holding that cake pan, trying to catch what blood she could but not quite understanding why she was doing it. The two young kids were a little horrified at the event and asked their mother, "Why did grandma want us to collect the blood?"

"She's collecting the blood for the blood sausage!" No doubt the image on their little faces was priceless as they decided, from that moment on, to never eat blood sausage again.

While my personal stories aren't as gruesome and horrific as some of the tales you are about to read, they are still little reminders about what life used to be like and how we all have a little "wicked" in our history, no matter how great or small. The stories in this book are sad, gruesome and sometimes worth a little chuckle. Enjoy or reel in horror while reading these true tales.

The Brutal Murder of Enos Lawrence

The dark angels must have been laughing over that house that night while the angels of mercy wept.

–Assistant Prosecutor Diekema

When the corpse of Enos Lawrence was discovered by Fred E. Noble and his wife while boating on the Black River, the bold headlines in the *Grand Rapids Evening Press* on April 20, 1896 read, "Horror At Holland." It was indeed a horror, as the crime committed was one of the most brutal and disturbing the city had ever witnessed in its history.

Enos Lawrence was a strong and muscular guy with a hot temper. He was forty-one years old and worked at the Holland Furniture Company. He and his wife, Alice had three children together—two girls and one baby boy. Alice had married Enos at the young age of sixteen. Enos was fourteen years older than she was, and she never really found herself happy with the life she chose.

In April 1896, Alice's brother, Raymond Coates, moved in with her and Enos. Raymond was from the Detroit area and had moved to Holland in September 1895 in search of some work. He found odd jobs painting and playing his violin around town, giving music lessons and doing housework around his sister's home, but the sentiment toward Raymond seemed to imply that he was a bit lazy when it came to finding a decent job. Enos had displayed irritation with the young man on more than one occasion, hoping that he would start to make better use of his time.

Photo of Enos Lawrence. *Courtesy of Charla Dumville Pfeffinger.*

Living with Enos and Alice wasn't all that great. Enos had a foul temper, and when he got upset, everyone knew it. Since Raymond had been living in the Lawrence household, he had witnessed numerous fights between Enos and his sister, and he didn't much care for the way Enos treated her at times.

When Enos suddenly turned up missing for a few weeks, townsfolk asked Alice where he had gone. "Oh, he found a new job up north, and we are packing and following him very quickly!" And in no time, Alice had sold everything she could that had once belonged to them, and she and Raymond took off with the kids. Everyone figured that she was telling the truth until Enos's body showed up in the Black River.

Enos had been missing for a total of three weeks. His muscular body was already deteriorating and grossly swollen when the unfortunate boaters came across his foot sticking out of the water. A coat was wrapped around his head, and his entire body was tightly bound with rope from his ankles all the way up to his neck. Metal parts from a reaper were tied to his neck in an attempt to weigh Enos down and make sure that his dead body never saw the surface again. His mouth was gagged with a leather strap that was tied so tightly around his head that it made his eyes bulge out. When the coat was removed from his head, a deep wound was discovered, exposing his brains. Police brought his body to his now vacant house.

The sudden disappearance of Alice and her brother made them the top suspects, and warrants for their arrest were sent out. The police up north were asked to be on the lookout for two adults with three kids. It didn't take long for a report to come back that the couple had been arrested and picked up by a sheriff in Kalkaska. Alice and Raymond had been renting a farmhouse there, living as husband and wife!

When news hit back home in Holland that the suspects had been discovered and that the brother and sister were posing as a married couple, people were sickened and outraged. Some even suggested lynching them. A huge crowd of more than one thousand people gathered at the train station in Holland in the hopes of catching a glimpse of Alice and Raymond. Names and jeers were being yelled by the crowd, and the police rushed them out of the train and into a police car as quickly as possible before the excited crowd turned too nasty. Early examinations got started right away, and Alice and Raymond were questioned separately. The story of a ruthless killing started to unfold.

A PERFECT NIGHT FOR A MURDER

It was April 4, 1896. Raymond was falling asleep in his room upstairs in the Lawrence house when he heard his sister and her husband start to argue. He heard Enos yell, "I will kill everyone in this house!" Raymond opened his eyes and listened for a while. The argument stopped, and he found himself falling back into sleep when the sound of his sister screaming awoke him for good. Raymond jumped out of bed and headed downstairs to find Enos standing over his sister with a knife, telling her, "I'm going to kill you!" Raymond's eyes darted around the room for a weapon and locked on to an axe leaning against the stove. Enos lunged at him. Raymond grabbed the axe, took one swing and landed it in his head. Enos dropped to the floor. Alice looked at her brother.

"Now what?" she said, worried. The night was chilly, and Raymond felt a cold pass through him. Maybe it was the spirit of Enos, whom he had just butchered with an axe. Dragging the lifeless Enos out into the night, he loaded the heavy body into a cart and started to make the trek to the river about eight blocks down the road. Raymond hoped that no one would be wandering about that night. He had a body to dispose of and didn't need anyone getting in his way.

He was sweating by the time he stopped the cart at a bridge over the Black River. He had strapped metal to the body in the hopes that it wouldn't surface. Raymond paused in the darkness before he tipped Enos into the dark water. He heard someone in the distance and thought that it could be a rig heading his way. Raymond's heart beat quickly as the sound dissipated, and he quickly dumped Enos into the river. A loud splash was the only sound heard as Enos sank into the murky abyss below.

Coming back to the Lawrence home, Raymond put the cart away by a shed and entered the house. Bloodstains were splattered here and there, and he

The two daughters, Abigail and Grace Lawrence. *Courtesy of Charla Dumville Pfeffinger.*

got to cleaning them immediately. When he was done washing his hands thoroughly, as if that would get rid of the crime, he sat down by the stove. He stared at the wall for a while, thinking about what he had done. Alice was nowhere to be found. Not wanting to disturb her, he went upstairs without talking to his sister and tried to sleep, but his conscience would keep him awake. Sleep would never come that night.

In the morning, the two daughters came downstairs, unaware as to the chaos that had happened the night before. The oldest daughter, Abbie, was the first to notice that her father wasn't at the breakfast table. "Where's Pa at?" she asked.

"He's gone away," said Raymond flatly. Alice was sitting at the table, and her face turned white. She looked away from everyone. He had spared her the details of the killing the night before, and Alice didn't ask for them, but they had to think quickly. Alice was in a panic. They were confident that Enos would be food for the fishes, but they had to come up with a good excuse as to where Enos went if people started to ask. They made plans to sell as much as they could for money, get out of Holland and head up north to Kalkaska as soon as possible. In the hopes of further covering up the crime, the two immediately went to Grand Haven and, under fake names, were married on April 14, 1896. They would have new identities and have the marriage license to prove it to people.

Alice and her brother thought that they had gotten away with it but were terrified when the police showed up a few weeks later at the doorstep of the farmhouse they were renting in Kalkaska. Raymond took off running but ended up turning himself in. The police had surrounded the woods, and he wouldn't have escaped. He later told police that he ran because "he thought he was going to get in trouble for breaking up his sister's marriage." He was going to get in trouble for that and a whole lot more. Alice and

Raymond claimed that the reason they got married was so they could hang the marriage certificate up on the wall—then there would be no doubt at all who they were to strangers. Alice figured that it would be a great way to cover up the crime and acquire different identities for themselves, but other people begged to differ.

Some felt that the brother and sister were actually in love and had killed Enos to get him out of the picture. For the people of Holland, the story was one of murder, brutality and now possibly incest.

THE TRIAL AND CONFESSIONS BEGIN

Anna Gillette had been a housekeeper at the Lawrence home to earn some extra money. When the trial began, Anna was called to testify and delivered a story that sent the courtroom into excited murmurs. Everyone around town was talking about the brother and sister who had run off and gotten married. Anna claimed that Alice and Raymond showed affections for each other that were unnatural. Her eleven-year-old daughter even testified that she saw the couple in "compromising" positions not suitable for a brother and sister. Anna said that Alice and Raymond would take "a morning nap together" and would shut the bedroom door when Enos left for work. The housekeeper claimed that she would see the two in intimate embraces and even said that she saw them sneak off into a woodshed in the backyard.

Alice's daughter Abbie stated during the trial that she had never seen her mother and uncle kissing and had never seen them go into the woodshed, nor anything else strange. Multiple residents and neighbors of Holland stated that Anna Gillette had a horrible reputation and wasn't to be trusted to tell the truth even under oath.

When John Witeveen was sworn in on the stand, he told the jury that Anna Gillette could be trusted. Another resident, Orlando Bottom, also swore that she could be trusted, as he'd known her for eighteen years. A handful of others testified that her statements could be taken seriously. Alice and Raymond continued to deny any type of physical relationship and said that they only got married to try and take suspicion off themselves up north. The defense tried to say that Anna Gillette was making things up by asking why the woman would continue to work there if she had witnessed incest taking place. Even two brothers-in-law of Enos stated that they did not believe the woman. Prosecutor Diekema tried to use this bizarre bit in the story to prove that "there was something more between Raymond Coates and

Sketch drawing of Alice Lawrence, *Ottawa County Times*, 1896.

Mrs. Lawrence than brotherly love." He hoped that their unnatural relationship would prove to be the reason they had planned the murder together. But it would seem, in the end, that Alice and Raymond really believed that getting married would help hide the crime they had committed.

Raymond played dumb about the murder for as long as he could but eventually caved in and told his version of the story to the courtroom, but something just felt wrong about what he was saying. Questions were asked as to the leather strap tied around Enos's mouth. Doctors felt that the reason for death was strangulation and not the blow to the head. Raymond claimed that he had no idea how the leather strap got there, as he hadn't done it. He said that he attacked him with an axe and that was that. Raymond didn't have any injuries from a fight, and the prosecutor used that evidence to prove that Enos was killed in his sleep or in some other condition.

When Enos was found, he was half-naked, and Raymond claimed that he had no idea what became of his clothes, or his nice watch for that matter, which Abbie remembered her uncle wearing, as she later said in court. She even testified that she had heard Raymond say he'd like to kill her father. It was also very suspicious that Alice supposedly didn't ask any questions about what had happened to her husband that night or the following morning. "My sister did not ask me any questions, and I did not answer any," was Raymond's response to that.

Something was telling the lawyers and people of the jury that these two had planned this out beforehand. This wasn't a case of self-defense or insanity, as Raymond's lawyers were trying to use. There were just too many things going against them. The metal buttons and buckles of Enos's clothing had been found in the ashes of their wood stove in the kitchen. Because Raymond committed perjury to get married to his sister, the prosecutor argued that he would do it in court: "In every aspect, these people were unnatural. A plainer case of murder has never been presented. I ask you to return a speedy verdict of guilty."

Raymond was the first in the trial to be sentenced by a jury, and as the verdict was given, Raymond's demeanor didn't change. It only took the jury half an hour to decide on first-degree murder. Raymond asked if he could say a few words to the jury before he got off the stand, but the request was denied. When he was brought back to the jail, someone in the crowd yelled, "Get a rope!" A reporter noted that Raymond didn't look around to see who had said it but just smiled. On August 19, 1896, Raymond was finally shipped off to Jackson Prison for a life sentence. It was now Alice's turn for judgment, and Alice wasn't ready to give in just yet.

ALICE'S TURN

Dr. Jared Wetmore was a playboy of sorts around Grand Haven and Holland. He had been a resident of Holland for ten years and had two children and a wife. He was thought to be handsome, well dressed and a man of good height and weight, according to descriptions of him. He was considered an excellent physician but had a penchant for the ladies, even though he was married. His poor wife put up with it, and there were always rumors that he and Alice Lawrence had a relationship on the side. So when Jared Wetmore left the state, leaving his wife and children behind shortly after Alice and Raymond were arrested, some wondered if he could possibly have been involved. Perhaps there was no way that small Raymond Coates could have killed and disposed of Enos Lawrence on his own. Someone else could have been involved.

Alice had already admitted that Raymond had killed her husband. She had said that Raymond didn't like him and didn't like the way he treated her and that he was going to end it. But in an effort to help reduce her sentence, Alice told the jury that Dr. Jared Wetmore had been the third accomplice in the murder.

Jared was shocked when the police arrested him. His wife was insistent that he was innocent, as were his friends and family. Jared claimed that the reason he was gone was that he went to assist in a difficult operation on his sister in Wisconsin and didn't even leave Holland until after Alice had made her confession about the murder on paper to the police. If he had been guilty, he probably would have left immediately after Enos was killed. Some suspected that Jared was out of state and following the trial through newspapers until he felt that it was safe to come back after Raymond had been shipped off to prison.

When Raymond was brought back from Jackson Prison to testify against his sister, he suddenly made mention of a mysterious man who just happened to be outside on the night Enos was murdered. He had no idea who he was, but his descriptions fit the image of Jared Wetmore. Not everyone in Holland had a good thing to say about Wetmore. Many said that "he had ruined more than one family" with his womanizing ways, and it was said that Alice wasn't involved with her brother, but rather with Jared—the mastermind behind the whole murder. It was brought out in court that Enos did, in fact, catch Jared at his home once talking to Alice; a huge fight followed that got the police involved.

Alice stated on the witness stand that she had known Wetmore for about seven years and had planned the murder with him. She claimed that during a conversation with Jared before the murder of her husband, Wetmore told her, "He always misuses you and always will as long as you live, and we might as well put him out of the way first as last." They talked about Raymond's dislike for Enos as well.

Alice said that Wetmore used chloroform to knock Enos out the night of the murder and that it was his idea to use the leather strap on Enos to make sure that the man stopped breathing, but Jared insisted that Raymond be the one to make the blow to the head with the axe. The involvement of Jared Wetmore in the case made sense, given his medical background and how the body was ultimately killed by strangulation. The strap in the mouth was thought to have been the note of a "professional" or someone who understood how the body worked a little better than Raymond Coates and Alice Lawrence.

Jared sat in jail for months before he was let go. For whatever reason, Alice later admitted that she implicated him in the crime to try and get a lesser sentence for herself by "confessing" and putting the blame on another person. Wetmore's lawyers did their job well and proved that there wasn't enough evidence to link him to the crime; with Alice's new confession that she had lied, Wetmore was a free man.

After he was acquitted, Jared Wetmore left the state and was never heard from again until a curious letter arrived for the county clerk in Holland in September 1904, wanting to know information about the doctor, as he was "making himself notorious" out in Oregon. But had Jared been involved? On the stand, Alice was solid in her confession involving Jared. When he entered the picture, much of the murder and details started to make sense. Did Jared perhaps threaten Alice somehow? Maybe threaten to harm her children if she didn't recant her statement about his involvement?

After a nineteen-hour deliberation by the jury on September 22, 1896, Alice was sentenced to twenty years for second-degree murder. She was sent to the Detroit Correctional Facility for Women. An angry article in the *Jackson Citizen* called Alice a "degenerate" and boldly stated "that as a girl she was untrustworthy, as a young woman she was reckless, as a bride she was unfaithful, as a wife she became a murderess and later, as a murderess she married her companion in crime, who was her own brother." The same article published a letter that Alice had written to her mother while in jail. She mentioned her religion a lot and that if it wasn't for her faith, she would have lost her mind—God would help her get through this. She mentioned crocheting lace for her daughter Abbie. Another letter in the article written by Alice's mother to a friend in Wisconsin noted, "I believed her guilty. She is neither insane nor irresponsible. You can imagine a mother's grief when forced to say this of her own flesh and blood, but it is true."

In 1897, Alice was seeking a pardon from the state to get out of the women's correctional facility in Detroit and to be able to take care of her three children, who had been living with various family members after the trial was over. She wrote a poem in the hopes of softening up the pardon board. It didn't work, and it is unknown what became of her or when she got out of prison.

Wedded to a man of 30
When a child of 16.
Thinking to be loved and cherished,
But alas, 'twas but a dream.
'Twas a dream that soon was ended
And reality came instead,
Filling my young heart with sorrow,
Disappointment, fear and dread.

Each day I kneel in my prison cell,
Where no sunshine enters in;
Must I forever thus go on
Suffering for another's sin?
And must my children's lives be spent,
No sister's love to know,
No mother's tender watchfulness,
Which none other can bestow.

Heavenly Father, wilt thou hear me
When I make this heartfelt plea?
Wilt thou cause our kind old governor
To come and pardon me,
So that I may have my freedom
And to my loved ones go?
May he have earth's richest blessings
On his journey here below.

The state pardon board opened an investigation on Raymond in April 1910. He had been in jail for fourteen years. By November 19, 1910, Raymond Coates was a free man and quickly married Mina A. Taylor in Grand Rapids. They moved to Battle Creek in a home on Fountain Street. So much for a life sentence! Raymond still used his musical skills to get by and make money, while his new wife was a candy maker. Census records show Raymond listed as a traveling salesman, and the family did move around the country from Arkansas to Texas.

It's hard for any reader to determine who to feel sorry for in this tragedy. It will probably never be known what everyone's true intentions were—was Jared Wetmore indeed involved and the mastermind behind the whole thing? Or was it just Alice and her brother looking to do away with a husband they felt treated her poorly? Was murder the only solution to solve all of their problems? We will never know for sure.

If He Can't Have Her, No One Will

Egbert "Happy" Dyke had been dating Molly Fleming for a little more than four years. She meant everything to him and was the only girl with whom he had ever been in love. He was a thirty-three-year-old car mechanic, ten years older than she was, but Molly always said, "I don't care about that! I just want you." And that was enough for Happy. They had met in 1920, and after two years of dating, the couple got engaged. They wanted to wait to walk down the aisle and take their time, but they had been having talks about saying "I do" sooner rather than later.

Happy never felt that anything was really wrong with their relationship. They got along well, and every Friday he would drive his 1917 Dodge touring car over to the Big Springs School in Conklin, where Molly was a teacher, to pick her up for the weekend and bring her home. During the week, Molly stayed with the Knauff family on their farm. The Knauffs were a huge farming family, and the longer Molly boarded with them, the more she got to know their oldest son, Edward. Edward was a budding farmer like his father and was proving to be very successful at it. Molly found herself developing a crush on the young man.

One night, Happy needed to drop off a one-hundred-pound sack of sugar for Molly's family. He pulled up in his car and tossed the heavy bag over his shoulder. The weight of the sugar was nothing like the weight that pressed against his heart when he saw Molly with Edward Knauff. Happy looked at her, confused. She was dressed nice, and they looked like they were getting ready to go somewhere.

"Where are you going?" he asked Molly, shooting a dirty look at Edward.

"I'm going to the dance with Edward. I'm not going with you tonight." And that was all she said. Not wanting to cause a scene, Happy said goodnight to her family, excused himself from the house, got into his car and drove away.

His fingers gripped the steering wheel tightly. What did this mean? Was it over? Was she actually dating this man? What did that young kid have that he didn't? Happy knew that Molly and he had their differences—age and religion being two big ones—but he wasn't expecting this. Happy didn't know how to take it. The love of his life was being taken to a dance by another man, and everything he had seen in his future was fading away. Hopes of a wedding, possibly a family, were all gone in one sudden, awful moment.

As the months went, Happy moved to Grand Rapids to try and forget her. Molly had told him that she didn't want to see him anymore and that she was engaged to Edward now, but she wouldn't be that easy to forget. Strangely enough, Molly continued to write Happy in Grand Rapids. Each letter would always be asking him to come back home and start over, noting that she still loved him. The letters were tormenting Happy because no matter what she said, Edward didn't seem to be out of the picture. Since the night he saw her with Edward, he had lost twenty pounds in only a couple months. Inez, Molly's younger sister, even tried to help the tortured Happy by giving him her opinion. "You need to just walk away Happy. She's not going to leave Edward," Inez told him.

But Molly kept trying to balance the two men in her life. She was comfortable with Happy, but Edward was closer to her age and something new and exciting. Happy wasn't Catholic, and that was a big issue with her family. There was always something about Happy she wasn't sure about. One newspaper described Happy as being "socially inept."

Love Turns into Rage

On October 17, 1924, Happy thought to himself, "I'm going to try one more time to make it work with Molly." He had been doing a repair job on a car in the area of the Big Springs School and knew that Molly would be finishing her school day soon. He pulled up to the school, walked up to the door and knocked. He was greeted by a sour-faced Molly, who exclaimed, "Happy, I'm not going home with you! I have another ride coming for me." Molly's friend, Henrietta, was at the school with her and later noted that

Happy looked really confused when Molly told him that she wouldn't go with him. Perhaps he was expecting a warmer greeting from the girl who had continued to write him.

Happy turned around and headed toward a woodshed on the school property. Once inside, he lit up a cigarette. Anger swirled in his mind like the smoke around him, and he was at his wits' end with her. Molly watched Happy enter the woodshed from the schoolroom window.

"I need to end this with him today!" Molly stated out loud. After the children were excused and the school emptied, she marched outside with Henrietta in tow. "I'm going to go end this affair!" Molly forcefully told her friend. Not wanting to be part of a lovers' quarrel, Henrietta wandered off to wait for her friend to finish her ugly business.

Molly stepped into the woodshed and saw Happy looking forlorn, smoking his cigarette. "I do not wish to see you anymore Happy! You need to leave me alone!" Henrietta could hear the couple start arguing with each other even at a distance. The yelling continued for a few minutes until two bloodcurdling screams pierced the air. Henrietta knew that they had come from Molly, and she frantically ran to John Zimmer's farm, the closest house, for help.

A small group of school kids still playing in the area also heard the screams. They bravely headed in the direction of the sound to find their schoolteacher lying on the cement floor of the woodshed, her head resting in a pool of blood. A bloody axe lay beside her. John Zimmer showed up to the scene not long after Henrietta ran off in search of him and carefully inspected Molly, finding a gaping hole in the back of her skull. He lifted the still breathing girl from the cold floor and took her to his farm. The police and doctor had been notified and were on their way to the scene, but there was nothing the doctor could really do for the type of head injury that she had. Molly died at about 10:00 p.m. that night.

The kids had witnessed Happy getting into his car and taking off as fast as the car would allow, and Henrietta knew exactly who Molly was talking to in the woodshed. There was no doubt in anyone's mind who killed her.

A Wanted Man

Happy was in a panic as he drove his car away from the girl he loved and had just killed. All he remembered was Molly coming into the woodshed and telling him that she didn't want to see him ever again. He remembered the arguing and his fist forming into a tight ball as she yelled at him to get out of her life. Everything was coming to a crest: Edward and her constant contact with Happy, as well as Happy's weakened mental and physical state. The last thing he remembered was his fist connecting with her head and then seeing her body crumple to the ground, not moving, with blood instantly pooling around her head. Or that's all his mind would let him remember.

After driving for some time, he pulled the car over to the side of the road, opened the door and ran into the woods. Grabbing a razor he had in his car, he headed into the depths of the thick trees and began cutting his throat. He felt the sting of the blade and the blood start to drip down his neck and chest. Looking at both of his wrists, he attacked each one with the razor. But fate would have it that he wouldn't be able to end his life that easily. The razor was dull, and no matter what he did, the right vein didn't get cut. Instead, he was left with nasty gashes and a bloody mess. Maybe deep down, he really didn't want to kill himself.

The police found Happy's Dodge along the road, the radiator still warm and the windows fogged up. He couldn't have gotten far, but he was nowhere to be found. The police wondered if Happy was heading toward Grand Rapids somehow to see his mother one last time before he killed himself. They set up dragnets in the hopes that they would catch their murderer.

Happy felt pain all over his body. The sun was setting, and the October night was getting chilly. He had been hiding under the stairs of the Marne

Happy escapes to the woods to end his life. *Original illustration by Amberrose Hammond.*

Police Station for hours. Dried blood clung to his neck and wrists. They ached from the razor blade he had used on himself earlier in the day with little success. The dull blades just cut the surface of his skin, and he really had no idea what he was doing. The police would come and go, their boots pounding on the wooden staircase above him, the officers totally unaware that the man they were hunting was literally right under their feet.

As the early evening settled in and no trace of Happy was found by the police, they started to believe that he had killed himself and was probably dead in the woods somewhere, given the horrible crime he had committed. When the police went home and the station was quiet, Happy slowly moved from his hiding place and headed out into the night toward the Marne Fairgrounds. Having a key to the grounds, Happy let himself in and started to wash the dirt and blood off his body, making some bandages for his cuts out of his clothing and splashing some cold water on his face. He knew that his life would never be the same again and had no idea where to go from here.

Happy knew that the police were already after him and that it would only be a matter of time before he was discovered. He was tired, cold and aching. Realizing that there was nothing more he could do to escape his situation, he decided to turn himself in and headed toward the house of Sheriff Danforth, whom he personally knew. It was early Saturday evening when Mrs. Snyder looked out the windows of the gas station she ran. Her eyes got large as she saw Happy Dyke walk past the station. She telephoned Deputy Sheriff Cole, who was nearby, and told him excitedly, "Happy is going up the road!" Three other men had also spotted the wanted man solemnly walking down the highway.

Deputy Cole showed up before Happy made it to the sheriff's house, and he made no effort to resist. He put his hands up and let the deputy arrest him.

"THE POOR FOOL"

Happy sat in the Ottawa County jail, not saying a word. The magnitude of what he had done was weighing on him something horrible. He was depressed. He felt sick to his stomach. He wouldn't eat and looked like a mess. Molly was dead because of him. The story about the tortured love of Happy Dyke had spread fast around the county and even out of state. Some even started to feel sorry for Happy, calling him a "poor fool." But others had a different opinion of Happy's true motivations. Molly had told her sister, Inez, that Happy had tried to threaten her before. Friends and family in Grand Rapids reported Happy stating, "If I can't have her…no one will." But the sight of the jilted man who killed his lover and the story behind it pulled at the heartstrings of a few.

On October 20, 1924, Happy's family and friends paid a visit to him. His brother, Joe, stepped into the cell and saw a shell of a man sitting there. He was bearded and sloppy-looking. "Buck up and take your medicine like a man," he said to him. The comfort and tough love of his family did well for him, but the anxiety of the upcoming trial was still to come and his fate to be decided.

The first examination began on October 28, 1924. Happy was brought into the courtroom, displaying no emotion. Henrietta and one of the schoolboys testified that Happy had been at the Big Springs school. The schoolboy stated how he had found their schoolteacher laying in the woodshed. Happy was up on a first-degree murder charge. As the trial continued, Happy finally took the stand on November 21. He was nervous as he sat down at the front of the courtroom. It was quiet and all eyes were on him. The courtroom was packed with curious people. He told everything starting from the moment they met to the night he saw her take off with Edward Knauff at her family's house. He talked about trying to let her go but how she kept coming back to visit him or would write to him telling him how much she still loved him.

On the day of the murder, Happy said that she came into the woodshed calling him "a devil and a liar and said she would not be seen in the daylight with him for at least two weeks." The meaning of this "two weeks" matter is unknown.

"I struck her twice, and then I don't remember anything else. I went into the woods, cut myself and the rest of the story is well known," Happy told the courtroom. He claimed that he had no memory of using the axe. He said it was her "jibes" and "taunts" that put him over the edge.

The only thing Happy's attorneys had to work with was temporary insanity, using his mental state to justify his actions and try and lesson the sentence. Testimony on the witness stand by a man named Roy from Conklin stated that Happy had told him, "I would rather see her in her grave than the wife of Ed Knauff." The prosecutor, Miles, asked, "Did you think his mind was unbalanced?"

"Yes," said Roy.

"Would you say he was crazy?" the lawyer asked.

"No, not crazy, but just crazy on this love affair."

The prosecution strongly felt that the crime was premeditated based on his previous statements to people, the razor in his car to attempt suicide after and even a bottle of carbolic acid that was never swallowed. When Sheriff Fortney took the stand, he said that he had known Happy for twelve years and knew that "Dyke had no malice in his heart for Molly Fleming."

When the jury finally came to a conclusion after many long hours, the verdict was manslaughter. Happy seemed relieved. It was all done and the charges were lessened. The judge warned the jury not to be sympathetic in their verdict, but the members stuck to their charge. The sentence would be seven to fifteen years in prison. Family of Molly were furious with the verdict, wanting to see Happy put away for life for what he had done to their beautiful girl.

Did Happy plan the murder? Why did he have the carbolic acid in his car and the razor? Or was it just a case of rage that compelled Happy to take his fist to Molly's head, as well as an axe that he doesn't remember using? Only poor Molly Fleming in her grave will ever know the answer to what made Happy Dyke commit such a horrible act upon the girl he loved.

The Ku Klux Klan in Ottawa County

The most dangerous weakness in a democracy...the uninformed and unthinking average man.

–John Moffat

No one really knew what to think when word of the Ku Klux Klan began to spread through Ottawa County. The ghostly white robes, pointed hats with black holes for eyes and the fiery crosses are still disturbing images in the minds of many then and now. The Ku Klux Klan was looking for fresh blood to strengthen its organization, recruiting members mainly from Holland and Grand Haven and dispersing its pamphlet, *The Fiery Cross*, during its second revival in the 1920s. Townsfolk in Grand Haven began to report dark figures moving on the sandy dunes of Dewey Hill every night across the waterfront. Curious onlookers stopped what they were doing and watched as a fiery cross was lit on top of the giant sand dune. The KKK had arrived.Who was behind this? What did it mean?

A Brief History of the Ku Klux Klan

The era after the Civil War, known as Reconstruction, was a difficult time for the American people. Billions of dollars had been spent on the War Between the States, and the South was left in shambles. While Abraham Lincoln abolished slavery with the signing of the Emancipation Proclamation, it

Early costumes of the first Ku Klux Klan. *Courtesy of Library of Congress.*

didn't solve everything for the African Americans who had been slaves for more than two hundred years. Racism ran deep in the South, and many of the white Southerners firmly believed that African Americans were inferior and were intended by God to be servants of the white man. The solution to the problem wasn't going to happen overnight with the end of the war.

The Ku Klux Klan was created in May 1866, just one year after the end of the Civil War, in Pulaski, Tennessee, by six men: John C. Lester, Frank McCord, Richard Reed, John Kennedy, Calvin Jones and James R. Calvin. It initially started as a secret fraternity club; the name came from the Greek word "kuklos," which means "circle." To make the name appear more mysterious, they modified the word to "Ku Klux" and added "Klan." Founding member John Lester felt that the words had an "occult power" to them and said, "The sound of it is suggestive of bones rattling together."

To gain new members, they started putting mysterious advertisements in the newspapers announcing what night they would be meeting at "the Den," the official name of any Klan meeting place. Some scholars feel that the Klan wasn't started solely with the intention of terrorizing the newly freed slaves. Newbery-winning author Susan Campbell Bartoletti wrote, "Some modern historians accept John Lester's account that the six friends formed the Ku Klux Klan purely as a social club and that the club then broadened into a racist organization that regulated the lives of black people. They claim little evidence indicates that the original Pulaski Klan bullied or seriously terrified anyone during the first summer of its existence." The men would

Early illustration of the Ku Klux Klan terrorizing former slaves. *Courtesy of Library of Congress.*

dress up in outlandish costumes reminiscent of ghosts. They would show up at parties unannounced and talk in crazy voices, and many considered them odd and entertaining.

They continued to organize themselves, coming up with strange names for membership positions. Members went by the titles of grand magi, grand cyclops, night hawks and grand wizard, and regular members were called ghouls, among other strange titles. It sounds like something out of a modern-day comic book. The group became highly organized and grew in numbers, and many members felt they were pressured into joining or flat-out threatened. New members would be initiated into the group with crazy ceremonies and were taught all of the secret codes. Most importantly, all members were required to carry out the group's orders and to always, above all else, stick up for and protect other Klan members no matter what.

As word spread of this freaky group of people roaming the countryside at night in white sheets, pointed hats and strange masks, African Americans also took notice. Their superstitions and beliefs led some ex-slaves to feel that these men were Confederate soldiers returning from the grave to exact revenge. Others knew to simply avoid these men at all costs. Ghosts or not, they were dangerous and were a real threat.

Nathan Bedford Forrest, one of the first major leaders of the early Ku Klux Klan. *Courtesy of Library of Congress.*

As the Klan transformed into an utterly racist beast, its goal became to "control" the ex-slaves. The Klan began terrorizing black families who had their own property and were trying to have a peaceful life. If the government wasn't going to let the South have its way, then they would take matters into their own hands.

The founders of the first KKK truly felt that they were vigilantes just looking out for people and their property. As the Klan progressed and organized throughout the southern states and became known as the "Invisible Empire," its leadership was taken over by Nathan Bedford Forrest, the Civil War general remembered in history for the slaughter of black Union troops at Fort Pillow, Tennessee. He was later pardoned by President Andrew Johnson for this heinous act. Nathan was a former slave owner as well.

In 1871, the U.S. government stepped in and passed a Ku Klux Klan act to help protect people from its malicious activity. The first incarnation of the Klan would eventually fizzle out until it was revived again in Georgia in about 1915.

THE KU KLUX KLAN OF THE 1920S IN OTTAWA COUNTY

The second incarnation of the Ku Klux Klan was going strong by the 1920s, stronger than it ever had during its first run in the 1860s. The Klan was gaining a major political influence over many states, not only with a racist agenda but also, this time, with anti-Catholic, anti-immigrant and anti-Semitic agendas—among other things with which the group didn't agree. The movie *The Birth of a Nation* by D.W. Griffith, released in 1915, was an important film and still is considered something of a gem in cinema history. The film did its best to make the KKK look like a truly American institution that was "good, just and patriotic" to its core. The movie was watched by millions and protested by millions more. The images of the hooded KKK members in the movie were made to look like heroes, and the second wave of the KKK was ignited with a fuel like never before.

When Michigan edition copies of *The Fiery Cross*, the publication of the KKK, mysteriously started appearing around Holland on random doorsteps in mid-August 1923, many townsfolk were alarmed. The large caption on the front page of the publication read, "Klan Wave Hits Michigan—Enthusiasm Sweeping the Wolverine State." The paper promised that because of the "enthusiasm," it would be publishing a weekly edition just for Michigan. There would also be editions printed for Ohio, Indiana and Kentucky. Burning crosses had already been lit in Kollen Memorial Park in Holland.

On September 18, 1923, the *Grand Haven Tribune* reported that the Klan had moved its way north from Holland and set its fiery eyes on Grand Haven with the burning of a cross atop prominent Dewey Hill, located on Grand

Haven's waterfront. People started to wonder if Ottawa County had its own Klan Den, but no one knew, or at least no one was talking. It can probably be assumed that one had been formed, given later research and discoveries, such as KKK membership cards with names of men from Grand Haven, Holland and Spring Lake on them.

The headline in the *Grand Haven Tribune* on September 25, 1923, was, "Burning Crosses on Dewey Hill Believed to Have Had Start at Hands of 'Kid Klan.'" Before the sun had set, the paper described black-hooded figures adorning the hill, preparing to light their burlap, kerosene-soaked cross on fire. Starting a week before the article was printed, a burning cross had appeared every night on Dewey Hill. The reporter mentioned that the crosses were getting less "cross-like" every night, and on the final night, it was more like an "overgrown camp or bonfire variety."

On Wednesday, September 26, 1923, the newspaper wrote of a meeting that had taken place the previous night, but no one had known the location. Rumors circulated that the meeting had happened in Duncan's Woods, a nice park along Sheldon Road in Grand Haven, but trying to spy on it wasn't "advised," according to the paper. Casual passersby found the usual amount of "snugglers" in the park, but no white-robed figures having a gathering.

A letter sent to the *Holland Sentinel* and published in the paper on October 1, 1923, from an "Ottawa County Klansmen," read, "They say we are an unlawful group who do not dare show our faces. They are unaware that we are among them daily and that our influence is felt in every act of the

Dewey Hill in Grand Haven, where KKK members lit their fiery crosses. *Courtesy of Loutit District Library.*

community." The paper chuckled at the fact that the man couldn't reveal his real name, but secrecy had always been a part of the Klan's ways. During 1923, the KKK enrolled about 141 men from the Grand Haven/Spring Lake area in only a few short months. The clan wanted to control as much of Michigan as it could and tried to set up groups wherever possible.

According to an article from the *Michigan Historical Review*, author Calvin W. Enders, KKK researcher and former professor at Central Michigan University, pointed out that "more than 160 Havenites and neighbors paid the klectoken [$10.00 dues] and swore allegiance to the lodge of the fiery cross. These klansmen, who resided in the Grand Haven–Spring Lake area were strategically placed to control the politics of northern Ottawa County." Enders also noted that the majority of the members of the Grand Haven Provisional Klan were from Grand Haven, with Holland members second and Spring Lake third.

Klan activity during the 1920s was running rampant in Michigan all the way to Detroit, the thumb and along the western shores of Lake Michigan. Michigan historians Bruce Rubenstein and Lawrence Ziewacz pointed out that Detroit was the main hub of KKK activity but that activity also flourished in "Flint, Saginaw, Bay City, Lansing, Kalamazoo, Muskegon, and the conservative Dutch communities along Lake Michigan were fertile recruiting grounds for the Klan."

An Indiana edition of *The Fiery Cross* from August 17, 1923, proclaimed, "MICHIGAN IS ENGULFED IN KLAN WAVE":

> *During the past two weeks, more candidates have been initiated than in any one month before, and applications for membership are increasing at a rapid rate. During the past week, 300 candidates took the oath of Americanism beneath the splendor of the symbolic fiery cross. From Niles, Dowagiac, Sturgis, Grand Rapids, Cassopolis, St. Joseph and other cities throughout the state come glowing reports of the progress being made.*

For such a colorful and violent history as the KKK is known to have, the local papers seemed rather relaxed about the presence of the secret society—or perhaps nervous. It's been speculated that papers in the area didn't want to give much attention to the subject for fear it would recruit more members just by constantly mentioning the group's existence in the area. Author John Moffat, who wrote a thesis titled "The Ku Klux Klan: A Study of the American Mind," stated that many of the people who were interested in the 1920s Klan had "small-town minds" and a "provincial fear of all things foreign." Many of the members who joined the KKK did so out of ignorance or fear, or both. They were also mostly blue-collar workers.

According to Craig Fox's book *Everyday Klansfolk*, other popular cities for KKK activity in Michigan were "Grand Rapids, Flint, Bay City, Jackson, Lansing, Kalamazoo, Saginaw, Pontiac and Muskegon." That's a lot of cities! The gist of Craig's work highlights how active the KKK really was in Michigan outside of the Klan-infested Detroit region in the 1920s. The Klan was much more active in American life than people knew. Craig's book goes on to illustrate "that the advance of the 1920s Klan across the Michigan landscape was part of a wider nationwide marketing drive, carefully planned and lucratively executed by a calculating KKK recruitment machine."

Klan membership in Michigan has always been surprising to its residents; many are unaware that the KKK ever existed near their front doors. There were more than ninety "klaverns" in Michigan alone during the 1920s KKK revival, and the 1920s Klan gained more than six million members nationwide but had lost ground quickly by 1926, never to see the same numbers in membership again.

The Notorious Boston Blackie

According to the rules of war, Folger should have died the day he was shot, but he has the constitution of iron.

—Grand Haven Tribune, *April 6, 1900*

On Tuesday, March 27, 1900, John VanToll rolled his eyes when the familiar figure of George Folger (aka Boston Blackie) opened the door of his saloon on Second Street in Grand Haven and looked around. Blackie was a regular tramp, stumbling around from town to town and not doing a whole lot with his life. He had just been let out of the Ottawa County jail that morning and decided to do what he liked to do best: drink.

Blackie sat down at the bar. John VanToll could already smell liquor on the tramp's breath, and he gathered that he had started drinking as soon as possible after getting out of jail. VanToll and Blackie had never got along well. Harsh words were said quickly, and it didn't take long for Blackie to start a nasty fight with the proprietor. The two got in each other's faces, and when Blackie found the opportunity, he slammed his fist into John's face, knocking a few teeth out. VanToll didn't want any more trouble with the tramp, so he quit fighting and told him to get out. Blackie took one last swig of his drink and headed out the front door.

Once outside, Blackie wasn't done tormenting poor John VanToll. He dug deep into his pants pocket and pulled out a pathetic knife that was missing its handle. Using the knife as if it were a club, Boston Blackie walked back up to the saloon and plunged his knife through the front window, proceeding to break other windows in the same manner. VanToll sat inside staring at the crazy tramp putting his fist and knife through his windows. He had no idea what to do with Blackie.

After Blackie felt that the windows were sufficiently broken to his liking, he staggered back into the bar and threatened VanToll with his knife, waving it around wildly. VanToll was prepared to protect himself and reached for a gun he kept behind the bar. He aimed the gun at Blackie and told him, "Get back…or I will blow your head off!"

Blackie was too drunk and angry to care and lunged toward VanToll. With a quick reflex, John fired the gun straight at Blackie's head; he crumpled to the floor and started writhing in agony. VanToll waited a few seconds to see if Blackie would get back up, but he just lay there in pain. John had shot him right in the head, and blood was already pooling around his broken skull. The left side of his face was hanging on by shreds, and his left ear had been blown right off.

Local townspeople heard the commotion and the sound of a gunshot. Before John knew it, he had a good-sized group of gawkers around his saloon straining their necks to see what was going on inside. The sheriff and his men showed up to find John in a panic and the bloodied body of Boston Blackie lying on the floor. They weren't surprised to find it was Blackie, whom they had just said goodbye to that morning at the jail.

"I did not kill that man! This was self-defense!" John blurted out to the police. He quickly went into the story of what took place and what led to the shooting. Blackie was still conscience and tried to say to the police, "I've been murdered," over and over. Two doctors eventually arrived on the scene and took Blackie to a back room, where they did what they could to stop the bleeding and determine the damage to his skull. After they bandaged his head, they put Blackie on a wagon and sent him over to the Kirby House, a local hotel. The doctors didn't feel that the wounded man would live much longer. The police took VanToll over to the station, along with his gun as evidence.

The bartender and a few other men in the saloon were witnesses to the whole affair and backed John up in his story of self-defense, and everyone knew that if the case went to trial, John would walk away without any problems. But the community as a whole was outraged. For too long VanToll's saloon had catered to the shady side, and this was the last straw. After the shooting, an article appeared in the *Grand Haven Tribune* titled, "Down With the VanToll Saloon!" and argued that the place had long been home to hobos, tramps and other elements of vice.

The following day, Blackie was still alive and breathing at the Kirby House. Doctors were amazed and wondered if the man could possibly make a full recovery. His head was in extreme pain, but he was able to eat some. His hands were bruised and swollen after throwing the hard punch at VanToll and putting his hand through the windows with his knife blade.

Blackie told everyone while he was put up at the hotel that his real name was George Folger. He originally hailed from Boston, hence his nickname, and he used to be a druggist in Cedar Springs before he took to drinking.

According to Blackie's version of the saloon fight, VanToll bet him ten dollars that he couldn't kick him. Blackie accepted the bet, and that's when the fight happened. Blackie won the bet, but the two men got to arguing. The other men sitting at the bar grabbed Blackie, threw him outside and locked the door. Blackie claimed that he broke the windows so he could get back inside. A witness stated that the two did seem to have some type of wager going on.

On April 12, 1900, Blackie was moved to Mercy Hospital in Big Rapids so that he could be better cared for. He astonished everyone with his slow but miraculous recovery. Everyone commented on his "iron will." Blackie stated that he swore off liquor from that point and was done drinking. He had a new lease on life after his near brush with death. He was in a good mood all the way to Big Rapids, smoking cigars. Hopefully, whatever became of Boston Blackie after that put him on a better path and off the streets.

Goodbye Grandma!

Fifty-three-year-old Mary E. Pierce was described by newspapers as a woman who ran "the household with an iron hand and kept her husband at her beck and call." She was known to be a vindictive and short-tempered woman who punished her children harshly, usually with a good beating if she felt they deserved it. While she was respected by locals as being "a very neat housekeeper" and "frugal and industrious," she tended to have arguments even with her neighbors. She and her husband, Levi, had lived on their farm at Tallmadge for decades, but it wasn't a total surprise to some when she was found on her kitchen floor, murdered.

Mrs. Mary Pierce had three daughters. Two of them were grown and already had children of their own, and her youngest, Mary Isora Pierce, was only thirteen and lived at home. It was summer, July 9, 1895, when newspapers around Ottawa County reported that there had been a "murder at Tallmadge!" Everyone was shocked because the two suspects in the murder were only children.

Mrs. Pierce's seventeen-year-old grandson, George Cheesbro, had come to live with them that summer, doing work around their farm. Little Mary I. Pierce already had an older nephew in George, and the two got along very well. It wasn't reported that Mrs. Pierce was ever particularly mean to George, but when her daughter Mary did something she didn't approve of, she got out her whipping cane and gave the little girl a few good lashings to set her on the straight and narrow again.

On the Monday morning of July 8, 1895, Mary was helping her mother wash the kitchen floor. In all seriousness, Mary told Mrs. Pierce, "You missed a spot." Mrs. Pierce, believing that her daughter was being sassy, grabbed her cane and started to hit Mary. She took it without crying. She was used to it. The grandson George, however, had a different opinion when it came to how his young aunt was treated by his grandmother. Mary was a good girl, and he was tired of his grandma's bullying ways and harsh treatment.

Screams Are Heard

That Monday morning, neighbor Mrs. Palmiter heard "shrieking and cries for help" coming from the Pierce home. She quickly grabbed her bonnet and headed over to the Pierce farm to see what was going on. She had heard plenty of nasty arguments before from the family, but these were the sounds of distress; something didn't feel right to her. Approaching the house, Mrs. Palmiter saw Mrs. Pierce's daughter Mary look out the window and quickly shut the curtains. Mrs. Palmiter knocked on the door and tried to get in, asking if everything was okay, but the door was locked and no one was responding. She stood there a bit, figured that maybe it wasn't any of her business and turned around to head back home. Worried that something bad had happened at the farm, Mrs. Palmiter kept looking out through her curtains at the Pierce house. It didn't take long for her to see young Mary walk outside and move toward her father in the fields. George was soon to follow and then took off in the other direction, toward nearby Berlin about two miles away, which is today Marne.

Levi had started work on the farm that morning at 7:00 a.m. and was out in his fields when Mary came up to him rather leisurely. "Father…Mother is dead in the kitchen." Levi dropped what he was doing and made a mad dash toward the house. Bursting into the kitchen, he knelt down by his wife and checked for a pulse. There was nothing. Levi looked around the kitchen and noticed that the floor looked as if it had just been washed minutes before.

"Where's George at?" asked Levi.

"He went to Berlin. But I saw a stranger running away from here not that long ago!" blurted Mary.

Dr. Chappell from Berlin was the first to view the body. He was suspicious after inspecting Mrs. Pierce and called in the police for a possible murder. She had been beaten and choked so hard that handprints were still visible around her neck. Her shoulders were badly bruised, and a nasty gash was on her chin. Suspicion was quickly cast on the daughter and grandson, and the questioning began.

Mary told the police that she had been outside repairing a fence with George when both of them headed back to the house. When they stepped inside, they were horrified to find Mrs. Pierce lying on the kitchen floor, apparently dead. The first curious statement from Mary was that George had come into the house at the same time she did but went to change his clothes and then left to pick up a registered letter expected in Berlin. Pretty strange reaction after finding your grandma dead on the floor.

Mary said that she hadn't noticed any blood in the kitchen until after she came back with her father. There was a metal rod next to the dead woman on the oddly cleaned floor. She told the police the same thing she told her father: a strange man had been seen walking away from their farm.

When George's testimony was taken, the stories were completely different. According to him, young Mary asked George to run over to Berlin to get her change and do another errand for her. George told the police that he had been working on the broken fence but that Mary was still inside the house and "nowhere near him" while he made the repair. He had tried to get into the house after his job was done, but the doors were locked for some reason, so he just took off to Berlin.

While telling their stories to the police, George was nervous but Mary stayed very calm. Both of them seemed strangely unemotional about the death of their grandmother and mother. As the police listened, it was apparent to them that the only two suspects were the young kids and that they were going to have to be kept at the police station for lockup and further questioning.

Dr. Vanderveen from Grand Haven was called in to examine the body. His conclusion was that "blows and strangulation" were the cause of death. On July 9, George caved in and confessed what had happened. He claimed that he killed his grandma and that Mary had nothing to do with it whatsoever besides being a witness to the murder and trying to help him cover it up the best she could. Mary and George continued to not show much remorse. Perhaps that's very telling as to what drove them to commit murder in the first place.

"She became angry over something trivial and came at me with a knife," said George. "I picked up a metal poker and struck her on the head and neck." Mary watched the scene happen but didn't do anything to prevent it. This was her chance out. No more beatings and harsh treatment from her mother.

After George confessed to the killing, Mary broke down herself. Mary said that she and her mother had been having a horrible fight. George heard the heated argument, entered the kitchen and, in a short amount of time, began attacking Mrs. Pierce with the poker. He then strangled her until she stopped moving.

After the violence was done and Mrs. Pierce was dead and gone, the two looked at the chaos around them. They immediately went to work cleaning up the scene to try and cover up what had happened. They washed the floors and did their best to wash the blood off Mrs. Pierce.

Police noted that Mrs. Pierce had been strangled so tightly that the handprints were seared into her skin and blood had clotted in her throat. George was a large teenager at 180 pounds and had "wrists as big as a boy's neck." George must have put every ounce of anger inside of him into that vice grip on his grandma's neck.

They moved Mary Pierce to the Muskegon County jail for lack of space and a suitable place for a little girl at the Ottawa County jail. She retold her story to a Muskegon reporter that she had been helping her mom wash the kitchen floor, commented on the "missed spot" and was beaten for saying it. That's when George came into the room and grabbed Mrs. Pierce, throwing her to the floor. According to Mary, George told her not to breathe a word of this to anyone and took off to burn his bloody shirt. That's when Mary, not knowing what else to do, went and told her dad that "Mom was dead in the kitchen."

Levi stated that it hadn't been a poker that had been used to kill his wife but rather part of "a buggy brace used as a stove hook that curved up" that did the job. He told one reporter:

> [The brace] *was turned up at one end. That end of it and two-thirds of it from the end was a mass of gore and I believe he must have thrust that end down her throat and twisted it around there. The blood was not all cleaned up either. They had scrubbed the floor, but the stain is there yet. I told them to leave that splash there on the door—told them to leave it there to show what had been done. I knew George was high tempered, but I never thought he would do this.*

Word eventually got to Mrs. Pierce's two older daughters about their mother's death, and at their request, Mrs. Pierce was exhumed from the grave so her daughters could see their mother one last time. The body must have looked awful, but it was important for them to see her.

On August 16, 1895, a jury convicted George of first-degree murder. People were happy about the verdict, but the two continued to say that the murder was never premeditated. In April 1901, Governor Bliss changed George's sentence from life to ten years based on good behavior. The state pardon board reviewed the case and decided that Mary and George had not planned the murder. He would be a free man on March 27, 1903. They felt the "punishment for the act was excessive." George would only have a couple more years to go, but he would never make it that long. George died from tuberculosis at age twenty-two on May 10, 1901, while still in jail.

On September 6, 1895, Mary L. Pierce was sentenced to the Industrial Home in Adrian, Michigan, for manslaughter until she was twenty-one. She was one of the youngest women ever convicted in Ottawa County's early history. Before Mary died in 1898 while at the Industrial Home, she again admitted that the murder had not been planned at all and that she had no reason to lie as she was on her deathbed. Mary died on July 10, 1898, at sixteen of tuberculosis and heart failure caused from it.

The Fury of a Lynch Mob

No one intimately acquainted with Dutch character could ever imagine that this quiet people could be lashed into the fury of mob rule.
—Holland City News, *September 9, 1909*

Lynching, Hanging and Capital Punishment in Michigan

The term "lynch" is a harsh word that brings up images of ghastly mobs with pitchforks and torches, ready to string someone up in a tree and watch them dangle and squirm until dead. In the United States, lynching is mostly associated with the South, slavery and organizations like the Ku Klux Klan, but Michigan had its share of lynchings, hangings and "near lynchings." Capital punishment was used in the state's infancy, usually by hanging.

Michigan's earliest hanging goes all the way back to the Detroit area in 1763, when a Native American woman who murdered an English trader was caught and hanged for her crime. Most of the recorded lynchings or hangings in Michigan's history came from Detroit from the late 1700s and into the 1800s, carried out by government orders. In 1846, the State of Michigan passed a law against capital punishment.

One of the earliest reported lynchings in Michigan is from 1866. A young eighteen-year-old teen named John Taylor was lynched after an argument took place over a very small amount of money. John was already considered "different"—he was a former slave from Kentucky and was mulatto, and he also served during the Civil War in the First Michigan Colored Infantry. Eventually, he found himself living near Lansing working as a laborer on the farm of Daniel Buck. After feeling like Buck had ripped him off in payment, John attacked Daniel's three daughters with an axe during the night. The police caught up with the young man and threw him in the Mason jail. Once word spread about what had happened, an angry mob formed, and close to three hundred people armed with weapons of all types stormed the jail, broke in and dragged John out, beating and yelling at him all the way to a big tree. While John did not kill the women of the Buck family, he injured them badly and admitted this once the mob started to question him. After getting their answer, the people promptly hanged John for his crime.

A "NEAR LYNCHING" IN HOLLAND

The *Holland City News* tells the story of "three tramps, two white and one colored," walking past the farm of Gerrit Vandenberg in Holland, August 1884. Forty-three-year-old Gerrit was outside tending to his property when one of the scruffy men stopped and asked him if he could spare any food. Gerrit looked at the road-weary men and decided that he could spare a few scraps. He gave the men some food, let them sit and eat and then told them that they had to move on when they were finished. The men tipped their hats at Gerrit and walked off. Gerrit went back to work.

Not long after the three men left, Gerrit heard a commotion going on in one of his fields. His sheep were making all kinds of noise, and he could hear men's voices. Walking and looking around his property, Gerrit spotted in the distance the same three men he had fed earlier killing his sheep. Knowing that he was outnumbered, Gerrit took off without alerting the men and ran in search of Sheriff John Vaupell. Gerrit led the sheriff back to his farm and pointed out the men who were busy stripping sheep of fur and meat.

The sheriff quietly walked through the field toward the men and took the three thieves off guard. The men dropped what they were doing and started to run away, but as the *Holland City News* put it, "the colored gentleman" pulled a gun out of his coat, lifted his arm, brought the aim straight in line with the sheriff's head and fired. At the sound of the gun being cocked, the sheriff moved like lightning but was still grazed by the bullet. He lost his balance, fell down a hill behind him and rolled into a ditch. The tramps figured that he had shot him, and they took off running as fast as possible, throwing the gun in the field. Not only were they common thieves, they could also now add attempted murder to their list as well.

Sheriff Vaupell got up from the ditch as quickly as he could and did an assessment of his body, making sure that he wasn't mortally wounded. He felt something wet on his neck and looked down at his hands: blood. He felt his neck again. The bullet went through the side of his neck and came out of the back near his spine. He was lucky he wasn't paralyzed. He was in pain but had a job to do and was going to finish it. Climbing back out of the ditch, he could still see the three men running. With the help of neighbors who were aware of what was happening, Vaupell and some men finally caught up with the criminals after a mile and a half.

The men were brought before Justice Brink and given their sentences. The two men who didn't shoot were charged with "petit larceny," and the man who pulled the gun on the sheriff was charged for "assault with attempt to kill." None of them denied the charges, and they were put in the Holland jail.

Word spread throughout Holland of the ruthless attempt to end the sheriff's life. Tales of the heroic sheriff and the people taking the three tramps down were on everyone's tongues, but the people decided that they wanted to take the law into their own hands on this one. This was their sheriff, and they weren't going to have three bums waltz into their town, get away with just some jail time and go on to be free men again at some point. The people mainly wanted vengeance against the one who shot at Sheriff Vaupell.

The jailers noticed a large number of people starting to gather around the jail. They seemed edgy and upset, many of them screaming toward the jail, directing comments at the three men inside. The crowd was growing, and two hundred people at least were soon standing in front of the building. The police waited and watched, knowing that at any moment the situation could turn ugly.

It was 1:00 p.m., and the jailers figured that they could sneak away to eat lunch. As soon as they were gone, the angry mob took full advantage of the situation. The *Holland City News* stated that "the rioters then fastened the doors and began battering down the building opposite the cell that confined the negro and had nearly succeeded in getting inside when officers placed the negro in another cell." Frustrated, the people continued to stand outside, yell, scream and ring the fire bell all night long and into the morning hours. The police moved the men to the jail in Allegan to escape the angry mob the next morning. The paper stated that "if it wasn't for the police there, a first class lynching would have taken place."

The Heartache of David Hawkins

There was murder in his heart and he carried a loaded double barreled shot gun to carry out that spirit.
–Grand Haven Tribune, *January 29, 1894*

"Annie, I'm going to go out into the woods for a while and chop some wood. I'm going to go a couple miles out, so I'll be gone for a bit," said David Hawkins to his wife.

"That's fine dear. I have plenty to do around the house," she responded.

David stared at his wife for a while. She had a beautiful face, and he had been proud to say "I do" on the day of their marriage a few years ago in 1892. David wasn't a young man anymore. He was fifty-five, and he felt blessed to have Annie in his life. Annie was only forty. She seemed to genuinely love him, but one of her major concerns when they married was if he had enough money. She always seemed to press the question of his finances, and David would just say to her, "I have enough to support a wife."

David kissed Annie's forehead and walked out the door. Annie walked over to the window and watched as her husband disappeared down the road. She figured that he'd be gone for at least a few hours. That would give her plenty of time.

It was a cool January morning as David left his house, knowing that he was walking away from much more. Rumors were flying around the tiny township of Robinson about his wife and Abe Ellsworth—rumors he didn't want to be true. His first wife and mother of his son had died while he was living in Texas for a time. The heartache was awful, and Annie was a newfound happiness he thought he could never attain again. They had moved to Robinson only last spring on Annie's recommendation, as her brother had once lived there and owned a store. The land was nice, and David knew that he could be a successful farmer there. He was tired of moving around and was ready to just sit still somewhere and call it home for good.

Recently, David and Annie had had a huge argument. David had some papers proving that he owned land in Texas, and he didn't want anyone to know about them, including his wife. His finances were his business, and he was more well off than he cared to let on. He locked the papers in a metal box and soldered it closed. Annie's curiosity was too strong. She knew that something important was in that box, and like a kid trying to resist a candy jar, she broke the box open to find out what was inside. When David found the box opened, he was furious with her, and according to the *Grand Haven Tribune*, this may have been the start of problems between the couple.

David continued on down the road, his footsteps crunching in the snowy, frozen ground. He made sure to walk past Abe Ellsworth's house just in case he was watching and waiting for an opportunity. This was day two of David's investigation. The day before, David had hid in his barn and watched his wife leave the house and head toward Abe Ellsworth's. The rumors were proving to be true. This second day, after passing Abe's house, he made sure to sneak back toward his house unnoticed by way of the country fields and quietly snuck into his barn. Looking out of a window at his home, David waited. His heart was beating fast, and his thoughts were racing. His breath came out in fast clouds in the cold January air. Today would prove it once and for all.

Time seemed to move in slow motion as David waited with dreaded anticipation. Finally, a familiar person was spotted walking toward his house. Abe Ellsworth approached his door and knocked. The door opened immediately, and Annie let the married man inside. David's heart sank to the bottom of his stomach. There was no doubt in his mind now that his wife was having an affair.

"Well, there's only one thing to do now," thought David. He let himself out of his barn and walked toward the house, his heart thumping with each heavy footstep toward the inevitable end of his marriage. Without giving warning, David opened the door and was greeted by the sight of Abe's arms wrapped around his wife's waist. The big smile on her face fell to the ground as she and Abe looked in horror at the figure of David standing in front of them with a cold, blank stare on his face. David dove at Abe, and the two men started throwing punches and words. Annie screamed for them to stop fighting.

It didn't take long for Abe to get out of the house as quick as possible. When the man left, David turned around and looked at his wife. "How could you" was all he could say.

"I'm sorry, David…I really am!" pleaded Annie. But David's mind was made up, and forgiveness was not part of it. She continued, saying, "Well, if this is how you are going to be, then I am leaving this house." Then, as if she were the victim, she walked out the door and out of her husband's life.

David was livid and mentally exhausted. He was a hardened Civil War veteran, but this was the last straw for him. There was nothing in his mind that could make this right except for doing something extreme. He headed toward Grand Haven in search of the sheriff and judge and reported the affair to them, hoping to press charges, but the men didn't feel that there was enough evidence to convict them.

"But I saw them in each other's arms! I've seen her go to his house, and the village people have been talking about it for a while!" David pleaded.

"I'm sorry, but there's just nothing we can convict them with. We need more concrete evidence." David wandered around Grand Haven for a while, feeling hopeless and lost. Would there be no justice for him? Walking into a store, he asked for a bottle of chloroform, gave the shop owner the money, pocketed the bottle and headed back home.

THE END IS NEAR

If the law wasn't going to do anything, then it was up to David to be the law. Four days after finding his wife with Abe, David woke up, got dressed and picked up his double-barreled shotgun. He loaded the gun up with number-four bird shot and marched out his front door in search of vengeance. His first stop was the house of Abe Ellsworth. Annie happened to be looking out of the window of Abe's house when something caught her attention: her husband walking toward the house with a shotgun in his hand. She screamed and ran out of the house. David recognized the figure of his wife running away.

"Annie, stop!" David yelled after her. "Annie, stop!" David picked up his pace. "Maybe if I shoot my gun, she will stop," thought David. He stopped walking and pulled the trigger. Nearby, Edward Rawlings was watching with open eyes as he saw David bring the gun to his shoulder and fire toward his wife. The bird shot sailed through the air, and Annie screamed in pain and dropped to the ground. David took off and ran toward his wife, bending down over her. Annie was rolling in pain, grabbing at her left side. Her clothes were peppered with holes from the bird shot.

Word spread quickly that David had lost it and was on a murderous rampage through Robinson, out for Abe Ellsworth's blood. A messenger found Abe a couple miles away and told him to "stay hidden if you want to live!" Terrified for his life, Abe went into hiding. Annie would be fine, but the bird shot left some nasty marks on her left side and face. David continued his search for the man who had ruined his life and was confronted by residents John Powell and Milo Hatch.

"David…put the gun down and stop this madness!" The men could tell that David had lost his mind.

"No!" David screamed. "Just get away from me and let me finish this! I can't control myself any longer!" David charged at the two men like an animal, chasing them around and firing his gun twice at them, some of the shot grazing their skin but nothing major.

William Foster, a burly store owner in Robinson, saw what was happening and ran home for his gun. He would end this before anyone got killed. He loaded his gun with buckshot and approached David with his gun raised.

"David…put your gun down and stop this before someone seriously gets hurt." But David was mentally gone, and something was very wrong with him now. William fired a warning shot, and when David continued advancing toward the men, William fired directly at David. His body collapsed to the ground.

The three men hesitated for a moment and walked toward David's body. He wasn't moving but he was still alive. The buckshot had only grazed his ear. There really was no reason for David to be passed out cold. But what the men didn't know was that David didn't plan on walking away from this day alive and had swallowed the bottle of chloroform he had previously bought before going in search of Abe Ellsworth.

David's body was taken to an empty store building and placed inside. Someone watched over him all night in case he woke up, but he never did. He died the next morning. Reporters swarmed over Robinson following David's suicide. The police really had no one to bring to trial. William Foster was just trying to protect other citizens, and his buckshot didn't even come close to mortally wounding David. It was the poison chloroform that did him in. Edward Rawlings, one of the witnesses, didn't think that David intended to shoot his wife when he aimed at her but wanted to just startle her to get her to stop running away.

When the wife of Abe Ellsworth was asked about the affair between Annie and her husband, she told the sheriff "in an honest, candid manner that her husband would do no such thing as he was charged with!" This made everyone in the town raise their eyebrows in shock; it seemed that Mrs. Ellsworth was the only one oblivious to her husband's womanizing ways. It was rumored that Annie hadn't been his first affair. But Mrs. Ellsworth was so convinced of her husband's innocence that she invited Annie Hawkins to stay with them after the death of her husband. The townspeople just shook their heads. The residents of Robinson Township didn't want anything to do with the troublesome Abe Ellsworth, so they formed a "law and order society" and told Ellsworth that "he had better move from the area or take the chances of suffering from a coat of tar and feathers." Abe chose to pack up and leave.

David was buried at Robinson Township Cemetery; just the last name "Hawkins" is the only remembrance of him in the cemetery records. The little village of Robinson had never seen anything quite like what unfolded that day, and many were on David's side and felt sorry for the man. They knew that he had loved his wife and that his outbreak didn't come from the heart of an evil man—just a heartbroken one.

Argument Over Cows Ends in Death

...because he was fired to blind, unreasonable anger by the lashing of a woman's words.

–Grand Haven Tribune

When John M. Seelman died, no one was notified. The police, Sheriff Dykhuis and the coroner knew nothing of the man's unfortunate demise. When a few weeks went by, and the sheriff learned of the bizarre way the man was found dead, he opened up a case and started to investigate. He was livid that no one had told him of the death. It would seem that tragedy was about to plague the Seelman family for the next few years.

On a September morning in 1901 in Chester Township, fifty-two-year-old John Martin Seelman was found lying on his barn floor behind one of his horses, with a hole in his skull. John was still alive and breathing, but the nasty injury in his head looked awful and he needed a doctor's attention. The men he had been out drinking with the night before carefully picked him up and brought him into his house.

As soon as the word "doctor" was spoken, John became angry and frantic, telling everyone that he didn't need a doctor and not to dare send for one. The injury to the frontal lobe of this brain, which controls emotion and personality, probably accounted for his suddenly erratic and illogical behavior regarding a doctor. His family knew that he needed the medical attention no matter what, and word was sent anyway. Two doctors showed up at about noon, and it took the strength of everyone in the room just to hold John down so the doctors could get a good look at his head injury and assess the damage. But how did John end up with this awful hole in his head? Was he kicked by his horse? Why was he found in his barn? What had happened the night before?

The doctors knew that the head injury was possibly fatal. The family tried to tend to the wound, but John died a few days later on September 19. His death certificate stated that he died from being kicked in the head by a horse and congestion of the brain.

When Sheriff Hans Dykhuis learned of the death, he was immediately suspicious. He opened an investigation on the death, and the details quickly fell into place. The night before John was found with a hole in his head, he had been out with his son, George, and a few other men. As the *Coopersville Observer* noted, they were having a "drunken spree in Conklin." They were seen having one drink after another. After partying it up in the saloons, the men headed back to John Seelman's farm. One witness noted that the men had stopped in front of their home and started to argue; a fight seemed imminent, but the men sorted things out and kept on walking. When they got back to the farm, the men all passed out drunk in the barn, crashing on beds made of straw. Anna Seelman, John's wife, came out to the barn after hearing the men return and tried to get them to all sleep inside. Her son, George, was the only one out of the gang who seemed somewhat sober. George and Mr. Ulmer followed Anna inside rather than sleep in the dirty barn. The rest of the men slept there.

The next morning, George and Mr. Ulmer went to check on the men, probably now hung over from the night before. They found their buddies Pat Finnegan and Mr. Baker still sound asleep. John was found sitting in a horse stall behind one of his horses with a hole in his forehead.

When police began to question all of the men involved that night, Mr. Baker said that he woke up and, through a drunken haze, heard John groaning and calling with a great effort and only half aloud, "George, George," the name of his son. Mr. Baker thought it sounded strange and wondered what was wrong with him but didn't think too much of it and passed back out.

Sheriff Dykhuis tried his best to uncover a murder, but after weeks of questioning and a doctor who strongly felt that John did, in fact, die from a kick to the head from a horse, the case was dropped and no charges were made against anyone.

Anna Seelman, John's wife, went on her own crusade and was furious with one of the saloon owners for supplying alcohol to her husband, who got "abusive and noisy" when he drank, and for selling liquor to her underage son.

It's easy to imagine drunken John, stumbling around his barn in the night, his words slurring, stirring one of the horses and, at just the wrong moment, taking a horse hoof to the head. Everyone was drunk and passed out, so if it was truly an accident, the only living thing that was witness to it was the horse that kicked him.

TRAGEDY CONTINUES TO FOLLOW THE FAMILY

It was Saturday, November 20, 1909. George Seelman was now twenty-six years old and was described as a "big, brooding farm boy," living on the farm of Josephine Faylor and her daughter, Edna, just three miles north of the village of Conklin. George was a joint owner with Josephine on some of the animals and farm equipment. He had also bought thirty acres of land from her to farm, not to mention that he had inherited some of his father's farm land when he had died in 1901.

Josephine was sixty and a widow, having lost her husband to an unfortunate accident involving a switch engine about six years earlier. Josephine liked George enough, but she felt that he was a touch on the lazy side and constantly pestered and nagged him to try and get him to do "more" with himself. She wanted to see him succeed, and seeing that he was engaged to daughter Edna, Josephine wanted to make sure that her daughter had a capable husband who could take care of her. Once George and Edna were married, the two families would have a sizable amount of good land and property with which to work.

But on that Saturday, Josephine's words "fired rather than inspired," wrote the *Grand Haven Tribune*, and George couldn't take it anymore. Before he came home that night from delivering potatoes in Conklin, George stopped at a saloon and had a couple of beers. George had a hot temper and was tired of the old lady constantly nagging and complaining. He didn't interpret her words as "coming from the heart." They had been having arguments recently over some cows they jointly owned. She wanted to sell them, and he didn't think it was a wise decision.

When George got home, the last thing he wanted to hear was Josephine telling him what he should and shouldn't be doing with the farm and his life. The two started getting into a heated argument per usual. Edna was home and listened to the two start squabbling again. It was getting old. She headed to the kitchen to try to break it up, but this fight wasn't going in the direction of their usual bickering.

According to Edna's testimony, she saw George toss her mother to the floor and wrap his hands around her neck, choking her. "Stop! Stop!" Edna screamed as she jumped between the two struggling people, her mother coughing and turning red in the face. She managed to separate them, and they all stepped back. It didn't take long for the two to start arguing again over the cows, and as Josephine turned around to leave the room, George picked up a shotgun leaning against the wall near him and fired the gun into the back of Josephine as she was attempting to run out of the house. Her body dropped on the front porch, dead.

When the police found her, the *Coopersville Observer* noted, "Her clothes were burned to her back, the charge from the gun having set fire to them." Horrified at what she had just witnessed, Edna ran out of the house for help. She knew that the problem had escalated beyond anything she could do. The murder took place at 7:00 p.m. on Saturday. The sheriff didn't get the news until 11:00 p.m. Having only a horse and buggy to use, it took the police three and a half hours in the pitch-black darkness of the country roads to get to Coopersville and then onward to Conklin.

News spread quickly of the shooting, and everyone figured that George had escaped and fled the scene, completely insane. Some suspected that he could still be in the house, but no one wanted to take the chance that an armed killer could be in there, waiting to shoot again. Even Sheriff Rice of Conklin preferred to wait for the other police to show up rather than play the hero of the night. A large crowd of local farmers and neighbors was gathering in front of the Faylor house, waiting for the police to arrive, take over the tragic scene and bring some justice to the situation.

Some braver men decided to start searching the surrounding woods for the deranged man in the hopes that they might find him hiding. Josephine's bloodied and burned body lay on the front porch like an actor on a stage for the group of spectators. No one touched her or got too close. Everyone was just waiting for the other police to arrive.

As soon as the other men showed up, Sheriff Andre and his men felt confident to start inspecting the house. The men had flashlights, or "battery flash lamps" as they were called. The *Grand Haven Tribune* put it best: "The officers prowled about through the dark home, already reeking with the odor of smoke, blood and burned flesh." There wasn't a sound to be heard. No one but Josephine appeared to be on the bottom floor. The men headed to the second floor, the wooden steps creaking beneath their feet. The beams of their flashlights showed a few closed bedroom doors down a hallway. With hearts beating fast and guns ready to fire, they entered George's bedroom.

George was lying on his bed in a pool of blood. He was passed out but still alive. The police shined their lights on the body and noticed a gunshot wound in his left arm and on the left side of his chest. He had obviously failed at trying to kill himself and had passed out from the loss of blood. The police speculated that he lost his nerve and didn't try a second time to end his life. Sheriff Andre poured "stimulants" down his throat to wake George up just enough to get him to jail. They hauled his injured and weak body in a wagon to Coopersville and put him on the interurban train to Grand Haven.

When George came to and was interrogated by the police about the awful crime, his only excuse was, "She wouldn't stop nagging me!" That had to be some very annoying nagging for George to pull out a gun and shoot his mother-in-law. He claimed that he didn't know the gun was loaded. The questions by police continued.

"Were you planning on marrying Edna?"

"I was going around with her some," replied George.

"Did her mother not want her to go with you?"

"She never said anything about that," George stated.

"It was about the cows you were fighting then? The girl didn't have anything to do with it?" asked the police.

"No. She just kept nagging at me and I just couldn't stand it any longer. That's all." It was as simple as that for him.

George was locked up in the Ottawa County jail and spent most of the time in his cell lying on his bed and starring at the ceiling. He didn't want to talk much the next day after arriving at the jail. He was in immense pain, but when asked, "Why did you do it George?" he continued to say, "She kept nagging, nagging me all the time. I couldn't stand it any longer; I told the girl [Edna] I couldn't stand it and I was going away. She was always nagging me because I wasn't doing more about the place."

George didn't have any visitors, and rumors were flying that his fiancée, Edna, had walked twenty miles on foot just to see George in jail, but officers said they hadn't seen her at all. She eventually made the trek out to the jail, arriving on November 24. The couple was monitored by officers. Edna broke down in tears several times during her visit. She was the only person to visit Seelman while he sat in jail. After visiting him that day, she went back to Conklin to attend her mother's funeral. Edna seemed somewhat sympathetic with George, but when it came down to telling the police what they needed to know, she told them that she had seen George load the shotgun before aiming it at her mother. Police told George that Edna had said this, and he didn't argue with them. In fact, George never denied the murder from the start.

George was arraigned on November 23, 1909. He didn't really have anything to say in his defense except for the fact she "nagged" him so much that he was literally driven mad by it. He tried to make pathetic excuses as to why he did it or how it had been an accident. For being twenty-six years old, George was very well off when it came to his property. He had a lot of land and stood to inherit more someday if he married Edna Faylor. As the story spread, people started to take pity on him. No one felt that he had the "face of a criminal," and a reporter from the *Grand Haven Tribune* described George as follows:

> *There is not the repulsiveness about Seelman that people usually feel when they look at a man who has taken human life in cold blood. There is not that desire to shrink away from him that one would naturally feel toward a man whose hands were stained by murder. There is rather a wave of pity for him in the court room. His face is not wicked nor criminal. There is rather a look of frankness about it. His features are delicate, almost effeminate and weak, but there is something in the face by which one can understand the unchecked, blind passion, which caused George Seelman to murder the woman who had angered him. All day he sits in court looking at his shoes, his wounded arm hanging at his side. What he is thinking nobody knows, but the thoughts, which are supposed to fill a murderer's mind are not reflected in Seelman's face.*

George's wounded arm hanging limply at his side would never regain full use.

It was brought out in court that George couldn't read. George's defense tried to use that to his advantage, saying that George was "mentally incompetent." But doctors who examined him said that his illiteracy was more likely due to a lack of education and not incompetency. There was an attempt by George's attorney, Charles Smedley, to prove that Seelman was "always dull minded and not exactly right." During the trial, the courtroom was filled with all kinds of people who knew George or Josephine in Conklin. Nothing new was brought out in the trial, but people hung on every word, waiting to find out if George would be a free man, committed to an asylum or sentenced to life in prison.

January 20, 1910, was the official start of George's trial. Charles Smedley from Grand Rapids was defending George, and the only thing he had to work with was the insanity plea. The man had already admitted to the murder, so insanity was the only thing that Smedley could try. Something had just snapped inside George when Josephine Faylor was arguing with him for the last time, and Charles would use that to prove insanity.

It took the jury seven hours to come to a decision after all of the details were heard. The jury members didn't buy into the insanity plea and called George "weak minded but not insane." George was sentenced on January 27 by Judge Padgham to fifteen to thirty years at Jackson Prison for second-degree murder. Defense attorney Smedley asked the court for leniency.

One of the unsung victims in his tragic story is really George's mother, Annie. Her husband, John, had died from the head injury in November 1901. In 1904, her sixteen-year-old daughter, Lizzie, died from kidney issues, and later on, her sister-in-law tried to commit suicide. Before her son killed his future mother-in-law, Annie had already checked herself into the asylum at Kalamazoo and spent the rest of her days there until she died in the 1930s.

George served the lesser part of his sentence and was in jail for less than fifteen years. When he walked out of Jackson a free man, Edna Faylor was still waiting for him, and the two got married on April 4, 1923, in Mason, Michigan. George was forty and Edna was thirty-nine. The two only enjoyed eight years of marriage, as Edna passed away in 1931. George died on September 8, 1966, at his home in Muskegon. He was buried at McNitt Cemetery in Conklin between his wife and the mother-in-law who annoyed him so much in life that he shot and killed her.

Magical, Magnetic Water!

There is magic in these waters most wonderful.
—Sheldon Magnetic Mineral Springs pamphlet, 1873

"The Saratoga of the West" was the name bestowed on Grand Haven after mineral springs were discovered by Willard C. Sheldon. According to old history books, "The magnetic powers of the water are so strong that by holding a common penknife in the flowing stream for a few moments it becomes heavily charged with magnetism and readily attracts steel." When doctors started touting the use of mineral water to heal the sick and cure various diseases, savvy businessmen got to drilling in their cities in the hopes of finding the liquid gold. Sheldon found his mineral spring in 1871 and opened the Sheldon Magnetic Mineral Springs, located on the corner of Fourth and Washington Streets in Grand Haven. The building was gorgeous and offered games like croquet on its well-manicured lawns, as well as other pleasantries of the time.

The latter half of the nineteenth century took a huge interest in a medical concept known as hydropathy or water cures. It was believed that through hydropathy, diseases could be cured and pain would vanish. A combination of hot and cold water was essential to the process. Every state was working on getting its own mineral springs for the express purpose of bathing in them for their curative properties, as well as for their ability to attract tons of visitors. The springs in Grand Haven claimed to have cured everything from indigestion to problems with the kidneys, gout and everything in between. The magnetic water was considered just short of miraculous and was the

Sketch of the Sheldon Magnetic Mineral Springs of Grand Haven. *Courtesy of Loutit District Library.*

start of Grand Haven's tourist industry. Hotels such as the Cutler House across the street accommodated the guests who came to be treated at the springs. Thousands of people flocked to the bathhouses while they were in operation, in need of rejuvenation, healing and perhaps a miracle or two.

In 1871, the same year the Sheldon spring was founded, the Spring Lake Magnetic Mineral Springs Company was started after discovering curative water underground in Spring Lake. The Spring Lake House was immediately built to accommodate visitors. Nearby Fruitport in Muskegon County also claimed to have found mineral waters, and the Fruitport Sulphur and Magnetic Springs Company was formed. The City of Holland had hoped to find mineral water in its land, as did nearby Grand Rapids, but nothing really developed. Plenty of well-to-do families and prominent men in United States history spent time at the various mineral spring resorts in Ottawa County. But did the mineral waters really cure ailments? Did they have miracle-like properties?

On a small level, sometimes just the rest and relaxation these resorts offered were enough to calm people down and get their minds off a world that was steadily becoming fast paced and hectic with the dawn of industrialization and everything else that went into the making of a modern world. The mineral spring houses usually offered different types of baths in which to experience the water. Taking sulfur baths could actually alleviate some joint pain and bring inflammation down. Turkish and Russian baths were saunas and steam rooms that would further provide some relaxation. Hot and cold douches involved putting water, sometimes with high pressure, on various parts of the body to attain certain curative effects depending on a person's condition.

Old photo of the Sheldon Magnetic Mineral Springs during its prime. *Courtesy of Loutit District Library.*

An old pamphlet advertising the magnetic waters in Spring Lake tries to convince the reader that just about any cure can be achieved, but it may take a few tries in the water:

> *In many cases—perhaps in the majority of instances—the use of the water for the first two or three days rather aggravates than lessons the symptoms of disease. Under such circumstances, it requires much courage for invalids to bear up and wait patiently for a favorable change. In this stage but very few of them can maintain their cheerfulness; they seem to be either apathetic or despondent; but when the change does come—and it comes gradually—when the evidences of the departure of disease and the return of health so accumulates as to be conclusive, it would gladden the heart of a cynic to watch the flash of pleasure and hope on faces which but a day or two before were distorted by pain and despair.*

All of the pamphlets advertising the curative properties of the magnetic waters in Ottawa County contained statements and testimonies made by users of the mineral springs, swearing by their curative properties. Magnetic mineral water wasn't the only thing offered to people as a surefire cure in the late 1800s. The world was seeing a new age in which the average person could take their health into their own hands with a little gimmick known as the patent medicine.

Fake Cures and Pestilence

While researching this book, I couldn't help but stop and look at the curious advertisements that were squeezed onto every page of the old newspapers. One ad claimed that it could cure your kidney woes. Another noted that it could cure any nervous disorder, and the list went on. What were these strange medicines, and did they even do anything?

The nineteenth and early twentieth centuries were a wild and dangerous time for medicine. It was still easy to catch something awful like typhoid, diphtheria or smallpox, or to die from a broken bone. If someone took sick, doctors were either too far away, too expensive or just plain terrifying with their sharp tools and seemingly medieval ways. Patent medicines, or "nostrums" as they were also called, were sold almost everywhere and guaranteed a cure for just about anything a person could suffer from. People didn't need a doctor—they just needed to self-medicate themselves. Thanks to clever marketing and the new concept of "branding" something, patent medicines became one of the biggest industries in the United States. Entrepreneurs would blend their mysterious ingredients and trademark their names so that no one else could use it. They wanted someone to walk into a store and demand a product by its name, not just by what it did. People were bombarded with advertisements in the newspapers, in stores, on their yearly calendars and almanacs and on the sides of buildings and rural barns.

Patent medicines were cheap, rarely helpful and, more often than not, were more life-threatening than whatever affliction a person was suffering from. Early ingredients in Piso's Cure for Consumption contained

Old photo from Grand Haven showing the inside of a typical grocery store where patent medicines could be bought. *Courtesy of Loutit District Library.*

"cannabis indica" (or marijuana), morphine and a good amount of alcohol. If your baby just wouldn't stop crying due to teething, you could grab a bottle of Mrs. Winslow's Soothing Syrup at the drugstore, and your baby would soon be out like a light. Not because the little vial of liquid had amazing medical properties, but because it contained morphine. Some soothing syrups for babies also contained opium, so of course, any amount given to a little baby quieted them down or just knocked them out cold. Advertisements for soothing syrups always showed images of happy mothers with their well-behaved children calm or asleep. Some medicines even claimed that they could cure cancer. Anyone using these medicines figured that they did *something* because they felt completely different after dosing, usually because of the narcotics contained in the mix. It wasn't uncommon for heroin, cocaine, morphine, opium and other harmful ingredients like arsenic to be mixed in with the "medicine." Even some dentists at the time used cocaine to dull the pain while they drilled and worked away inside of some poor soul's mouth.

During the patent medicine craze, there were no advertising or ingredient regulations. It was a total free-for-all that made a lot of men

Left: If your husband took to drinking a little too much, a wife could slip him some of this medicine in his coffee and keep her fingers crossed. *Grand Haven Tribune.*

Below: Nerve Berries, another hopeless cure for that "lost vigor." *Grand Haven Tribune.*

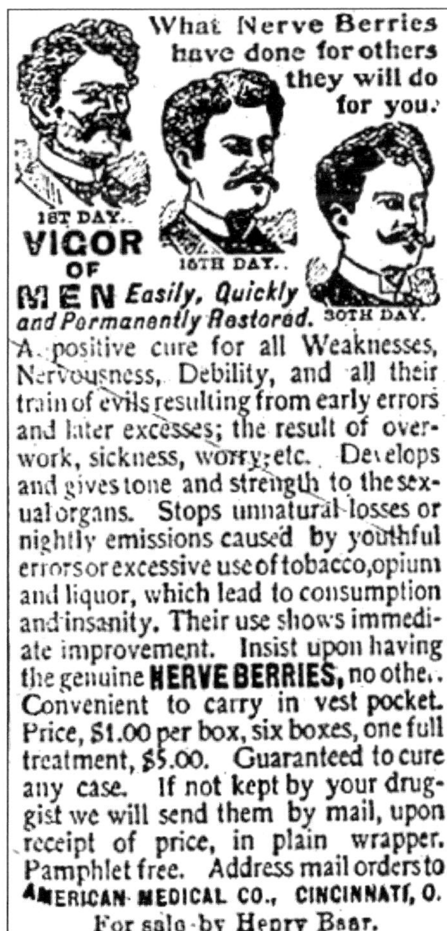

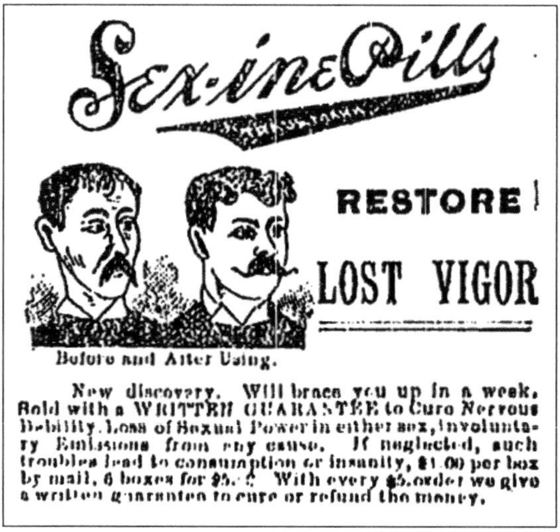

Sexine Pills could cure any man of "Lost Vigor!" Old advertisements like this were abundant in newspapers. *Grand Haven Tribune.*

very rich by poisoning ignorant people. Locals could visit any number of drugstores within Ottawa County and find these medicines in abundance on the shelves. They could read testimonials in their local newspapers from average people just like them, describing how they were cured. The claims were sometimes vague, such as Hibbards' Herb Extract ("For the Blood") or the brand Moxie, which claimed it was for a "vigorous life." Hood's Sarsaparilla "makes the weak strong." The effects of adding marijuana, cocaine, heroin, opium and laudanum definitely produced a result—one to which many got extremely addicted.

After the Civil War ended, a lot of men started to use patent medicines to cure their wartime memories and woes. This addiction to the patent medicine became known as the "army disease." The high amount of alcohol in most of the patents also kept people coming back for more. Even women who were anti-liquor found nothing wrong with "dosing" with a patent medicine to restore a little lost "vigor." Author Ann Anderson pointed out in her book *Snake Oil, Hustlers and Hambones* that "at one time, more alcohol was consumed by patent medicines and their mixtures than regular drinking. Some patents had 40 percent alcohol."

Patent medicines even prayed on mental problems like panic attacks, anxiety and sexual problems in men. If you were a man who had "lost his manhood," there was a patent medicine that claimed it could restore it. Most of the advertisements would have a sketch of a man looking ragged and defeated, but as soon as he started taking that medicine, the next drawing showed him bright-eyed and bushy-tailed.

Not All Patents Were Horrible

Lydia E. Pinkham's Vegetable Compound was a common household patent medicine around Ottawa County and the entire United States and can still be purchased to this day. In her time, Lydia Pinkham was one of the most famous faces in the United States. It's estimated that more than $40 million was spent on advertising her product, which always featured a picture of herself. The medicine was targeted toward woman and their "female complaints." Lydia had made her own "home brews" for a long time and gave them away to friends and family. Her "remedy" was a botanical blend, and everyone in her neighborhood swore by it. When Lydia's husband lost his real estate business in 1873, it was suggested that she start bottling and selling her medicine to make some money. The plan worked, and before the family knew it, Lydia E. Pinkham's Vegetable Compound was a smashing success that eventually grew into a factory hiring 450 workers.

Early medicine found its successes in advertising and careful wording. The Pinkham family worked hard on mass advertising, and Lydia wrote many of the ads herself until she died. One hilarious example goes as such: "A Fearful

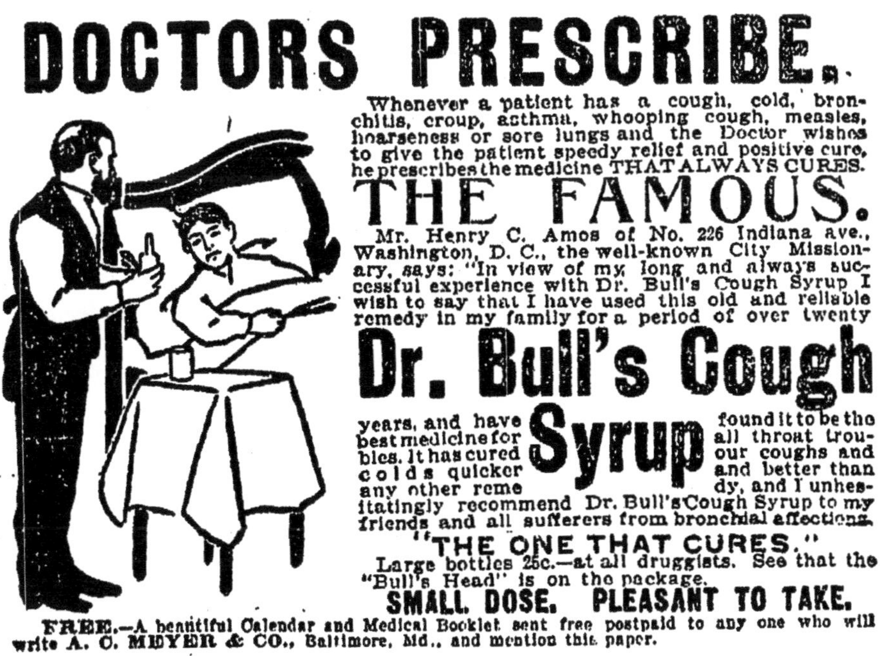

Coughing has always been a nuisance for the human race, but Dr. Bull's claimed to cure that problem. *Grand Haven Tribune.*

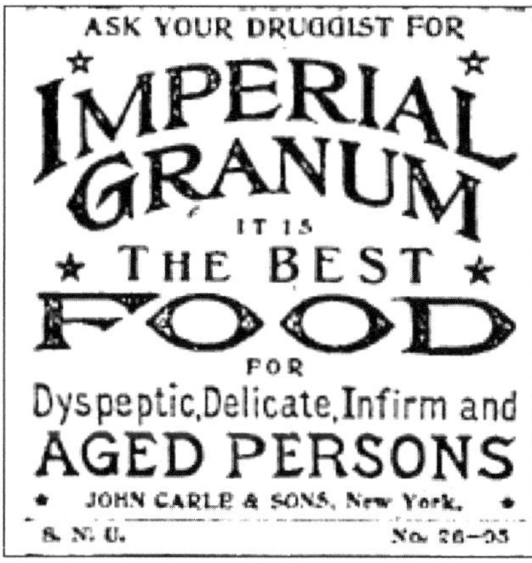

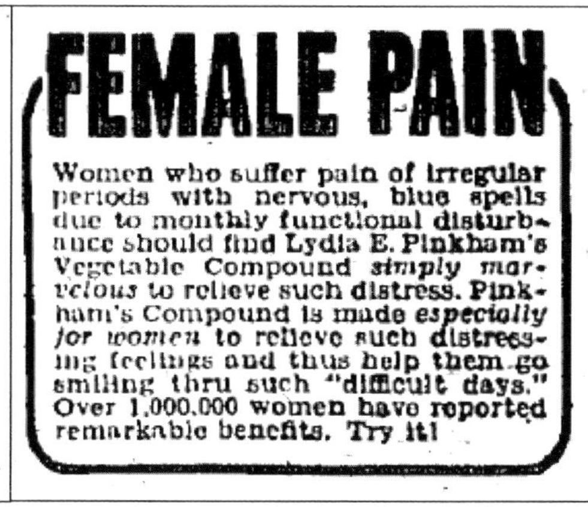

Above Left: While this was not a toxic patent medicine, this old ad displays how hilarious marketing used to be when it came to treating old age. *Grand Haven Tribune.*

Above Right: Lydia E. Pinkham's Vegetable Compound was said to help all women with their "female complaints." *Grand Haven Tribune.*

Below: Old advertising card describing the health benefits of Lydia E. Pinkham's Vegetable Compound. *Author's collection.*

tragedy. A Clergyman of Stratford, Connecticut, killed by his own wife. Insanity brought on by 16 years of suffering with female complaints the cause. Lydia E. Pinkham's Vegetable Compound, the sure cure for these complaints, would have prevented the direful deed."

Other than scaring everyday people with advertisements like that, Lydia created a pamphlet called *The Pinkham Guide for Woman*, designed especially for women and describing their complete anatomy and what to expect from puberty, conception, birth and menopause. Women adored Lydia because she had a no-nonsense approach to her writing and advice in a world where "female complaints" were usually swept under the rug and never talked about or taken seriously.

THE END OF AN ERA

The uncontrolled amount of poisons and narcotics on the market eventually led to the Food and Drug Administration in 1906. In 1911, the FDA published a publication called *Nostrums and Quackery* that strongly abhorred remedies like Mrs. Winslow's Soothing Syrup in a chapter simply called "Baby Killers." These "quack" doctors and makers of medicines were being exposed for what they were putting in their tonics, and people started to smarten up to the dangerous and addictive effects of them. The newly formed FDA also cracked down on the industry's false advertising and claims, making it illegal for something to be a "surefire cure."

In today's world, we have all of the same silly types of "cures" and quick fixes. They might not be filled with opium, morphine or cocaine, but they still

Patent medicines came in bottles of all shapes, sizes and colors and are quite collectible today. *Photo by Amberrose Hammond.*

claim to help you lose weight, focus better or give you the energy you need to work hard all day long. Our advertisements still falsely portray people with the use of photo editing and clever photography. The more things change, the more they stay the same.

When Disease Took Over

In the past, all kinds of strange and awful diseases could be the death of someone. Smallpox, tuberculosis, typhoid or even a simple injury could send someone to his grave. Medicines, medical procedures and vaccinations were still pretty primitive, and contagious diseases were taken very seriously. If they weren't, a town could have an epidemic on its hands. Some of the early epidemics were quite sad, as in the case of the Shield family near the tiny village of Agnew, which is located by Port Sheldon Township today.

Starting about September 26, 1894, a tiny blurb in the *Grand Haven Tribune* read, "Diphtheria has appeared in malignant form in Agnew. There are two cases in the family of Mr. Shields." When diphtheria (sometimes known as black diphtheria) came knocking, it was commonly known as the "strangling angel of children."

To catch diphtheria, one just had to be next to a person who had it. Starting in the lungs, diphtheria is a nasty respiratory disease. It causes a serious swelling of the lymph nodes in the neck that is very noticeable. It can affect a person's ability to swallow and even breathe. If left untreated, the disease moves on to affect the rest of the body, including organs such as the heart and kidneys. The first successful vaccine wouldn't be produced for another two decades. The feeling of hopelessness that must have accompanied the awful illness once caught must have been unbearable, knowing that once you had it there wasn't much else a doctor could do. It was also very easy to just pass it on to your family and friends.

Pauline Shield was a widow. Many of her children still lived with her, ranging from ages eight to nineteen. After getting news that her twenty-three-year-old son who had been living in Chicago had died of diphtheria, the family packed their suitcases and made the long haul to Chicago for his funeral. What they weren't expecting was the terrible fate that awaited the entire family after arriving home. Almost immediately, everyone took sick with the infectious diphtheria. Neighbors quickly shut themselves inside their homes, not wanting to come outside for fear of the disease. The papers warned to take great care around the family. Many of the family died within days of one another. Eight-year-old Edith was the first to die, on September 26. Bertha, age sixteen, died four days later on October 1. A week later, nineteen-year-old William died on October 7, along with his fourteen-year-old sister, Matilda, on the same day. Pauline had lost five of her children within a month's time. Not a single person was allowed to attend the children's funerals. The fear of contamination was too much to risk.

Smallpox was another nasty disease that cut short the lives of many in Ottawa County. The 1870s saw a large number of deaths due to smallpox, and in Georgetown Township, there was a special cemetery put aside just for victims of the disease. When the Shield children were buried, they were placed in a special spot called the Pest House in Grand Haven, located where the North West Ottawa Hospital is today.

THE PEST HOUSE

When someone became sick with a deadly and infectious disease, they were sent to places like the Pest House in Grand Haven, which was kept secluded and away from the general population so the disease wouldn't spread to anyone else. A trip to the Pest House meant that you were never leaving. According to local historian David Seibold in his book *Grand Haven: In the Path of Destiny*, the Pest House was rediscovered when the North West Ottawa Community Hospital added a new addition in 1969. As digging started, three tombstones were dug up with visible names and dates. The tombstones belonged to members of a family who died of smallpox in 1871. After the Pest House stopped being used, the area became a baseball diamond—it is just a little creepy thinking of little kids playing on top of the bodies of people who died from infectious diseases. When places like the Pest House were not in existence anymore, practices of quarantining became common. Eventually, vaccinations were discovered for many of these awful diseases, and the threat became nonexistent.

THE COUNTY POOR FARM

When someone hit that ripe old age where they just couldn't take care of themselves any longer or when a particular handicap made it difficult to live alone, a person could go to the Poor Farm, or County Infirmary (or Farm), as it was also known. The Poor Farm was located near Eastmanville, and the land for this property was purchased shortly after the Civil War. According to David Seibold, "Those who lived at the County Farm were referred to as inmates and it was rumored they were whipped to keep them in line." In 1880 and 1885, two investigations were opened on the Poor Farm that looked into how the "inmates" were being treated. This was probably one of those places that had plenty of rumors always circulating about what went on there with the elderly people, especially when they were called "inmates."

The Poor Farm had its own cemetery to bury anyone who passed away while living there. For a long time, the cemetery sat abandoned and hidden behind tall grasses. Only four tombstones remained as reminders of the people buried below. Wanting to preserve and restore the memory of the people who had to live at the farm and who died there, Marjie Viveen and Eldon Kramer started a restoration project. Through their hard work, they discovered (with the help of subsurface imaging) where the bodies were buried and how many there were in total. Each body was marked with a stone in remembrance. If people who died at the Poor Farm weren't picked up by their families or buried in the cemetery, they were donated to the University of Michigan Medical School and became cadavers for students to learn from and pick apart.

The Wrath of a Husband

The most unusual scene of mayhem ever perpetrated in Michigan.
—Grand Haven Tribune

At thirty-six years of age, Thomas Mahan was a hardworking man. He had a wife, children and a job that demanded that he be away from home a lot. His absence left his family feeling a bit abandoned at times, especially by his wife, Leona. Thomas was considered one of the best marine divers in the state, doing underwater construction, recovering objects and even bodies. Thomas had worked hard his whole life, and by the age of fourteen, he had already been operating a pile driver and helped drive the piles for the first Ferris wheel at the historic 1892 Columbian Exposition in Chicago. He started diving at the age of seventeen, following in the career path of his father. He was also a member of Company F during the Spanish-American War.

Thomas's long leaves of absence and his excessive amount of working to care for his family started to cause problems in Thomas and Leona's marriage. When Thomas was home, he stayed in the apartment upstairs in their home on Fulton Street in Grand Haven, and Leona lived downstairs with their three young children. They had gotten married at St. Patrick's Catholic Church in Grand Haven on September 23, 1899, and had been married for almost fifteen years, but their marriage was hanging on by a thread. Leona had threatened divorce on numerous occasions, and the strain and stress was growing on Thomas like an unwanted weed.

THE OTHER MAN

Fred Allison was a young all-star in the area. His father was the well-known tavern owner of the Nunica Bar nearby. Allison was a talented baseball player and made it to the minor leagues, giving him a few bragging rights about town. Thomas considered the Allison family friends of his, but something inside Thomas was telling him to start watching his wife a little closer and to keep an even closer eye on Fred Allison.

On April 14, 1914, Thomas put a plan into motion that would change his entire life for better or for worse. He had been spying on his wife's activities behind her back, and he was sure that he would get the complete evidence he needed if his plan worked.

"Leona, I'm going out for the night to work," Thomas said at about 9:00 p.m. Leona wasn't surprised because that's all he did anyway, but she knew that she could use the free time to her advantage. Thomas slipped out of the house and into the night. Leona waited for a while to make sure that her husband was gone. Confident that he wouldn't return, Leona let Fred Allison know that her husband had left for the night and to come over.

Thomas left the house knowing exactly what was about to happen. Thoughts of how he would handle the situation raced through his mind. Deep down, he hoped he was wrong, but he knew better. While spying on what his wife was up to, Thomas had visited the Hotel Lawrence in Muskegon and discovered the names "Leona Mahan and Fred Allison" as guests on the hotel register. There was no doubt in his mind what was about to happen. The only unknown outcome was how he was going to handle it. Thomas had found a spot in the shadows in the neighborhood, where he waited, giving Leona time to make her big mistake. Sometime between 10:00 and 11:00 p.m., Thomas started to walk back toward his house.

Thomas casually entered the home to looks of shock and horror from both Leona and Fred. "I'd like to know what you are doing in my home and with my wife," Thomas asked Fred. The nineteen-year-old Fred was speechless. He sat in terrified silence, while Leona tried giving excuses to justify Fred's visit. It didn't matter what excuse Leona was trying to concoct, as there was only one thing on Thomas's mind: bringing Fred Allison to his basement. Leona started to protest, and in a rage, Thomas dragged Allison down the stairs and got to tying Fred tightly into a chair. As Leona protested around him, Thomas kicked her in the back and sent her flying to the ground. Leona screamed and acted more hurt than she was. Worried that he had injured her badly, Thomas stopped what he was doing with Fred, picked his wife up off the floor and laid her on a cot. She acted as if she were in awful pain in the hopes of taking the focus off Fred. Leona finally blurted out, "Untie him! Can't you see the ropes are choking him?" Thomas was quick to realize what Leona's motive was, and enraged at her sentiment for Fred, Thomas forced Leona back upstairs and onto the front porch, where she sat in a panic for a bit.

Thomas Mahan was a powerfully built man, an athlete who had won a number of "ring fights" in his day. Fred was athletic, but he was no match for Thomas. Fred was sweating with fear but told the angry husband, "Tom, I deserve whatever you give me." Thomas would have liked to have taken a gun right to the boy's head, but that wouldn't teach a lesson; in fact, that would give him an easy way out. Fred watched as Thomas pulled out a mallet and chisel. Sweat from his forehead rolled into his eyes and stung.

"How could you do this to my family, Fred," cried Thomas. "How could you do it? Didn't you think of my little Tom, my two little girls?" After an hour of letting Fred panic, tied to the chair, Mahan went to work with his mallet and chisel, making sure that Allison would never commit the act of adultery again. The *Grand Haven Tribune* wouldn't come out and state exactly what Mahan had mutilated out of decency, but the polite phrase was, "Fred Allison and his 'member,'" so the modern reader today has a pretty good idea of what "member" means. The headline in the newspaper read, "Binds Victim to Chair; Mutilates With Chisel."

Halfway through the chiseling, Thomas stopped. Fred was nearly passed out from the pain, and there was blood everywhere. Thomas's oldest son was upstairs probably wondering what on earth was happening. The reports don't really say where the other children were at this time. Mahan asked his twelve-year-old son to fetch the doctor and not to come into the house. Little Thomas ran for the doctor and alerted his father when he saw the doctor coming down the street. Leona had moved to a woodshed in the backyard and was hiding. From the cracks in the doors, she saw her husband step outside and say to himself, "What have I done?"

Dr. Presley wasn't prepared for the gruesome scene that awaited him in the basement. Fred lay there in the chair, writhing in agony from the pain. Mahan told the doctor, "Finish the operation." Dr. Presley quickly told Mahan that he had to go back to his office and get more surgical instruments to finish the task at hand.

The doctor scurried out of the basement and, once at his office, grabbed his revolver and contacted another doctor and the police. When Dr. Presley arrived back at the Mahan house, Thomas started to threaten the doctor and told him that he had better finish what Thomas had started. The doctor pulled the revolver out of his pocket and pointed it at Mahan. The tables had turned, and Mahan quickly surrendered the situation over to the doctor and the police, who were arriving on the scene. Mahan willingly went with the police, and Fred was taken away to the hospital, where it was discovered that his wounds were not as bad as they had first appeared, but he would be in pain for quite some time.

Fred Allison Sr. was furious and stated, "Give me five minutes with this man Mahan and you can gamble that it will not be necessary to hold him for any charge." Young Fred had always had a good reputation around the town, and he was the "pride of his parents." Little did everyone know that he had been sneaking around with an older, married woman.

The Trial Begins

When the trial started, it was regarded as "one of the most sensational cases known to Michigan courts." The trial didn't start for months, but on November 21, 1914, when Leona Mahan took to the stand to tell her side of the story, the crowd waited with bated breath. The Ottawa County Courthouse was filled with curious listeners. Leona had been silent throughout most of the ordeal, while her husband had been the main target of newspaper headlines and town gossip since April. The people really wanted to know if she had cheated on her husband with Fred, who was more than ten years younger than her.

Leona felt that she had nothing to lose. If she was going down, she would bring other people down with her. She was tired of her situation, so she told her story bluntly and without any shame. Leona said that she and Fred had been living as "husband and wife" in Muskegon, which was confirmed when Thomas found their names on the register at the Hotel Lawrence. After Thomas confronted her about the affair with Fred, Leona left the house in search of work in Grand Rapids with thirty-nine cents in her pocket. There's no mention of her children and who was taking care of them. Not having much luck, she begrudgingly came back to Grand Haven. Leona had admitted to the affair with Fred, but what really put Ottawa County on its toes was when Leona brought the good sheriff, Hans Dykhuis, into the story.

Hans Dykhuis was considered an honest, hardworking man. He had been sheriff for a long time and was a married man. There was no way that he could be tied into this whole messy affair, but Leona sat on the witness stand baring all of the juicy details. In October of that same year, Leona had approached Sheriff Dykhuis and asked him to get Fred out of the state. "You have until 3 o'clock tomorrow to come to an agreement," Leona told Hans. The sheriff wondered if he was possibly being threatened by the woman but shrugged it off as nothing. When the sheriff did nothing to get Fred out of jail or the state, Leona put her next plan into motion. Leona had told her husband that she had had an affair with Hans as well, so in a later statement from Thomas, he mentioned that his wife had told him that she and the sheriff had met up on April 10, 1911, as well as a few times between December 31, 1913, and April 14, 1914. The people of the county were horrified that such accusations about their sheriff were possible, and friends and family immediately showed their support for Hans. Sheriff Dykhuis felt that the charges were nothing more than "a malicious spite against him" and that it was nothing more than a case of revenge on behalf of Leona.

Leona took the stand to testify against the sheriff on January 7, 1915. People were packed into the courtroom and standing on tiptoes in the hallway outside the courtroom to make sure that they heard all of the juicy details Leona was going to expose about her and Sheriff Dykhuis. Leona sat on the stand for more than an hour, giving all of the sordid details about her affair with Hans. According to reports, "The testimony had outdone even the extremist rumors."

Leona spent that hour explaining all of the places she had sexual relations with the sheriff, including meeting in front of a Catholic church and at the Ottawa County jail, and how she was paid on three occasions—ten dollars twice and five dollars one time—for services rendered. Hans supposedly gave her boy, Thomas, twenty-five cents to go buy candy with while he and Leona snuck off. Leona mentioned that she withdrew her membership from the Catholic church during the spring of 1914.

According to Leona, they discussed getting Allison out of the state to avoid charges after a late night visit to the jail. She gave him until 3:00 p.m. the next day to comply. When Hans ignored her request, she gave a letter to the sheriff's wife about their torrid affair, with all of the details, and also threatened to tell her husband of the affair. Adultery was against the law in those days, and the courts had to take Leona's story as the truth until proven otherwise. Deciding that he had heard enough for one day, Justice Dickinson closed the session and said that the case would resume on January 14. After hearing her story, many people felt that there just wasn't any evidence to support it, and the *Tribune* noted that "her story was too strong," meaning it felt like she was making it up.

So was the sheriff having an affair with the wild Leona Mahan? Was he trying to cover up a big mess he got himself into when he started paying Leona for "her services"? Or was Leona simply using the sheriff for revenge for him not helping get her lover, Fred Allison, out of the state? The sheriff was held in high regards. He was a good, law-abiding and married citizen—or perhaps so he wanted people to think.

The case continued to get pushed further and further back until it was finally on the August term of circuit court of 1915. Judge Orien S. Cross presided over the courtroom, as a decision would hopefully be made in defense of or against the sheriff. Prosecutor Osterhous dismissed some of the jury, which probably made the case a little more balanced and fair seeing that the sheriff had helped pick the first batch of jurors himself.

Charles E. Smedley, a lawyer from Grand Rapids, was called to the stand and asked to talk about a particular conversation he had with Hans Dykhuis. The lawyer refused to talk about it and used his "privilege as an attorney" to stay silent. Did he know something that would be damning to Dykhuis?

"But you are not Dykhuis's lawyer," stated the defense.

"I am any man's attorney, whether I charge them for legal advice or not," retorted Smedley.

Prosecutor Daniel F. Pagelsen attacked Leona's past hard, showing evidence of her filing for divorce from Thomas Mahan from a few years earlier. Her reason for divorce was that Thomas had threatened to "blow her up with dynamite or shoot her." She admitted on the stand that she had exaggerated that part a little. With that move, the prosecutor was doing a good job proving that Leona was prone to lying already.

"The trial is attracting many spectators, all of whom are men," the *Grand Haven Tribune* noted. "While the nature of the testimony offered yesterday by Mrs. Mahan is unprintable, ultra-sensational features have thus been far and few. Her story was merely sordid and immoral." Women were not even allowed in the courtroom to listen due to the "racy" testimony given by Leona, but the men hung on her every word.

On August 6, 1915, newspaper headlines in bold font read, "Judge Cross Orders Verdict of Not Guilty in Dykhuis Case." The sheriff was exonerated and cleared of all charges. The *Tribune* writer was very passionate about the whole case and hilariously stated, "The court room full of male spectators, who for two days have listened to the very essence of filth belched forth from human lips, lips of the sex from whom American manhood has been taught not to expect such things, were struck speechless at the spectacle of the public prosecutor declaring his belief in the innocence of the man on trial." Even the lawyer prosecuting the sheriff admitted that he felt Hans was innocent and quit. The entire courtroom was sobbing in relief. The people clapped wildly in defense of their sheriff.

"It was to the spectator like the experience of coming back again into the sweet clean world after a flounder in the filth and mire of the underworld," the writer went on to say. The men who came to hang on every immoral word were "given a new angle on life. It was to them like passing from the foul, tainted air of an unclean place into the pure freshness of God's out-of-doors."

On August 10, 1915, Leona sat defeated in front of Judge Cross as she was told that she'd be serving a sentence of nine months to three years at the Detroit House of Correction.

Thomas and Leona had three children, ages twelve, ten and five. As Leona was taken to Detroit for her sentence, the children rode with her and were dropped off in Ionia, where Thomas had found a place for them to stay closer to him. Reports of the kids leaving their mom noted that "[t]here were no curious spectators to witness the pathetic departure of the woman whose recent trials in Ottawa courts surpass all Grand Haven records for the brazen baring of a woman's very soul."

Thomas had been the first to be sentenced, on December 28, 1914, and was given one to ten years hard labor at Ionia Prison. At the prison, Thomas became a trustee and was able to work outside. He was liked by the warden, which also gave him an advantage at the prison. During August 1915, the Michigan State Pardon Board was already busy in Grand Haven getting the opinion of people in regards to pardoning or paroling Thomas so that he would be able to properly take care of his children. The three children happened to be visiting their father in prison when members of the parole board came walking through and found the situation pulling at their heartstrings. Thomas was able to get his job as a government diver back without any problems. When he went into prison, he was given a one-year furlough. On August 19, 1915, Thomas was paroled. He had spent a little more than eight months at Ionia for his crime.

Thomas admitted that his failed marriage was in part because of his intense work schedule. He worked around the clock and away from home a lot in an effort to support his family and see to it that his oldest son was able to get schooling someday and make something of himself. He even admitted that Leona continued to tell him things that were never brought up in court—there was no use in bothering to say them now because she was already locked up at the Detroit House of Correction.

Capt. Thomas Mahon Dies at Age of 96

Capt. Thomas Mahon, 407 Fulton, died at North Ottawa Community Hospital Sunday night. He had been in failing health for several years. Capt. Mahon was 96 years old. He had been residing at Spring Lake Trailer Park recently and was taken to the hospital by ambulance from there.

He was born Aug. 23, 1872 in New York City.

He was a member of Co. F in the Spanish American War and worked with marine construction and submarine diving for many years.

Capt. Mahon gradually drifted away from the sea, but never quite severed the bond. He was a retired sea skipper, sailing for 75 years, and was a deep sea diver for much of that time.

HIS INTEREST in the sea began at the age of 14 in 1886. His first job was operating a pile driver. Soon he moved on to Chicago, working along the waterfront, operating pile driver equipment on land and water. He also sailed on schooners hauling slab wood from Muske-

RETIRED LOCAL DIVER, Capt. Tom Mahon shown at age of 82 when he went down at Holland to complete laying a cable in Lake Macatawa.

Thomas Mahan's obituary from the *Grand Haven Tribune*.

On September 29, 1915, Fred Allison was finally sentenced to Ionia Prison for six months to three years for the act of adultery. He was escorted to the prison by Sheriff Dykhuis, who talked to the warden to secure a better housing arrangement for the young man. Many were shocked as they figured that Fred would get off the hook with a slap on the wrist. But it didn't take long for a petition to start up just one month later on behalf of Fred Allison to pardon him. The petition letter read that with the maiming of his "manhood," he had already been made to suffer enough and that prison wasn't going to do him any good. Of course, Fred was eventually pardoned and didn't have to serve that much time at Ionia. Shortly after he was let out of Ionia, Fred took off to fight in World War I for a year and a half. He got married in 1930 and moved to New York for a time, until coming back to Nunica to take over the Nunica Bar from his father for a few short years.

Thomas Mahan lived a long life and died at the ripe old age of ninety-six. He eventually remarried and had children with that wife as well. He built his own boat with a friend called the *Ramona* in 1921 and operated a tugboat called the *Tee Zee Lee* in the 1940s. At age eighty-two, Thomas finished a job laying underwater cable in one hour after a young man quit because he couldn't do it. He eventually acquired his own boat and construction company. His obituary is written proudly and noted: "Capt. Mahan was a powerful man, not too tall, and prided himself on his ability to work circles around men many years his junior. In his younger days, he had quite a reputation as a fighter and most men who tested him regretted the challenge."

She Was Found Swinging in the Wind

A search party was formed when Zelma Hammond's mother discovered a note:

> *Dear Mother and All—I am off for good. You need not look for me as I will not be around here. And do not blame Morris—that trouble we had a year or so ago. I am in same fix now with same fellow as before. Morris is straight. You can't blame him that I take this course. Zelma.*

A second note, seemingly meant for Morris Attwood, her boyfriend, read:

> *I am going away tonight for good, so good bye. The fellow I want is here after me now. That little trouble I got you into was not you, but the other fellow. I am very thankful for the money that* [unintelligible]. *Forget me and be happy. Zelma Hammond.*

Were they suicide notes? Was she just leaving the area and moving away with some other man? The rumor going around was that Zelma and a man she was seeing had a falling out. It was assumed at first that heartache was the cause of her disappearance and then, apparently, suicide. Zelma's mother felt a lump in the pit of her stomach after reading the notes and alerted the police. Call it a mother's intuition. The handwriting didn't even appear to be her daughter's. Neighbors and friends didn't really believe the suicide theory either.

When the sheriff and his men arrived on October 25, 1913, they started to search the nearby woods around Zelma's house. Halloween was just around the corner, and autumn leaves crunched under the officers' feet as they searched for clues. Halloween would come sooner than later, as they discovered a scene out of a horror movie. The limp, lifeless body of the thirty-four-year-old Zelma was hanging from a large tree branch just ahead

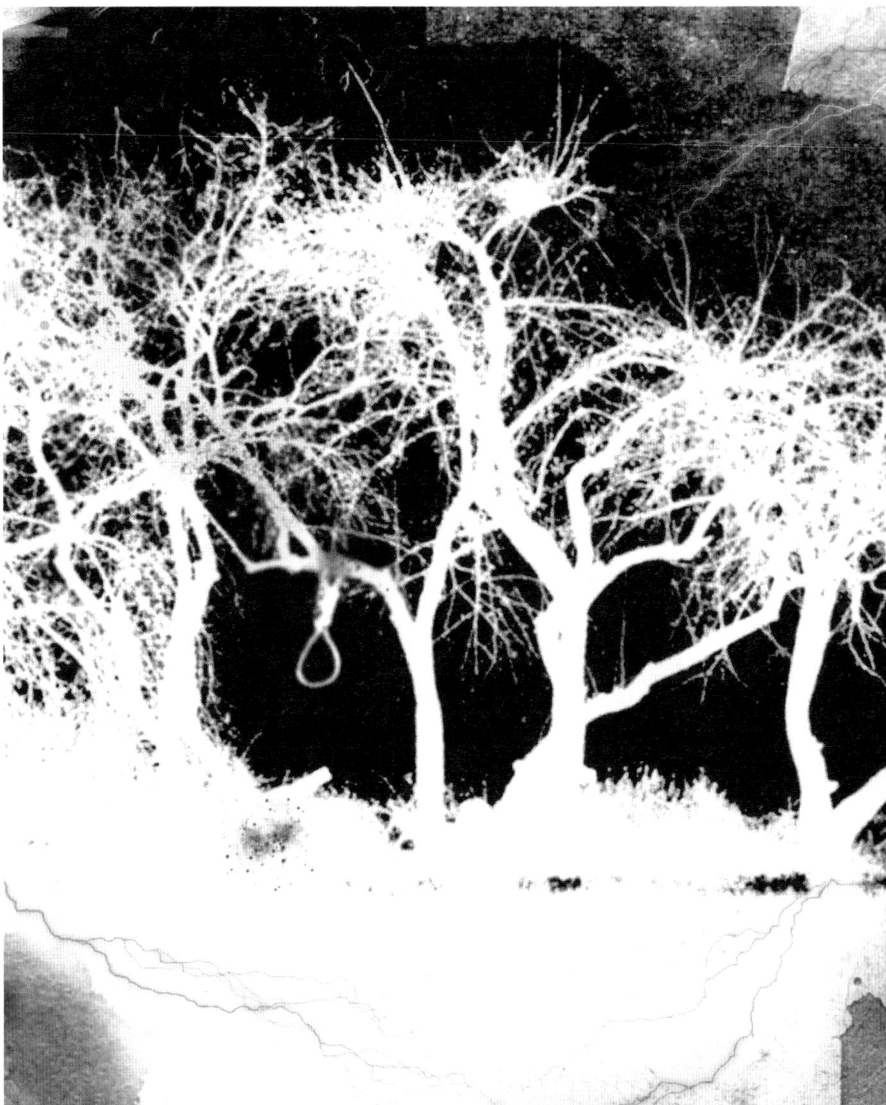

Original illustration by Amberrose Hammond.

of them. Her body slowly and quietly swung back and forth from her noose. Her tongue was protruding, and her fists were tightly balled at her sides.

The officers cut her down, careful to preserve the tree branch and rope as evidence, and brought the body back to her mother's house. The mystery of her disappearance had been solved. Clearly it was a case of suicide. Case closed. But Zelma's mother insisted that something wasn't right. "Zelma can't even tie a clothes line correctly, let alone tie a complicated noose to hang herself from!" she told police. They took her objection to the suicide theory seriously, and the likely suspects were gathered, namely the man Zelma had been dating (and, as it turned out, was secretly married to): Morris Atwood.

The police immediately went to the Atwood farm in Blendon Township. Morris and his younger brother, Frank, had heard the news of the possible murder of Zelma and didn't even seem surprised when the police showed up at their farm. Earl Smedley was left in charge of the Atwood farm as the two men were escorted by Sheriff Dykhuis and Deputy Sheriff Northouse to the Ottawa County jail. Morris was extremely calm about the situation and knew without a doubt that the police would come for him because of his connections with Zelma. They had already made preparations with Earl Smedley beforehand to watch over their place while they were gone.

The crime scene was ripe with clues, and the police started to investigate. First, Zelma's body was only six inches from the ground, and there was not much around from which Zelma would have stood to tie a knot and make the final jump to her death. There was a block of wood that police suspected could have been what she used. The knots around her neck were described as "too intricate for a woman to tie." Zelma didn't know how to tie a double-hitch knot. It was usually a knot that a man or a sailor knew how to tie. A store clerk from Georgetown was able to "identify the rope as one he sold to a particular man," and it was learned that the rope and the block of wood came from the Atwood barn. The two brothers even openly admitted that the items belonged to them. The double-hitch knot had been found in other ropes inside their barn as well.

ZELMA'S COMPLICATED LIFE

Zelma had eloped with her first husband, Guy Hammond, on April 10, 1901, due to the fact she was pregnant. They had one child together, but the marriage didn't work out and the couple was divorced. On January 7, 1903, Guy was ordered to appear in front of Judge Wolcott in Grand Rapids for not paying a temporary alimony to Zelma. By February 20 of the same year, he was thrown in jail after still not paying anything. In June 1903, Guy was out of jail and ready to be put right back in as he still had not paid anything to his ex-wife. Zelma told the court that Guy had put property in the hands of his uncle, William Hammond, to hang on to. Zelma went after it. Needless to say, her first marriage was frustrating, and she found herself falling into a similar situation again with Morris Atwood. It's not known for sure, but it appeared that Zelma started dating Morris and got pregnant again. She told Morris that it was his, which he didn't believe, but to avoid a scandal, they secretly got married in the juvenile court in Grand Rapids.

Her secret marriage was verified by Probate Judge C.E. Higbee of Grand Rapids, who testified that the document showing that Zelma had secretly married Morris on April 19, 1912, was genuine. Zelma told the judge that she had a child in March 1912 and that it belonged to Morris. Where the child ever went to is unknown. It may have been put up for adoption. The *Grand Haven Tribune* wrote that Zelma "was a girl below normal in intellect, easily led by those she took a fancy to."

As the secret life of Zelma was spilled out in the courtroom and reprinted by newspaper reporters all over the county, the trial was considered "sensational," and everyone was dying to hear all of the details concerning the case. The courthouse was packed with people everywhere.

The first evidence brought forth in the trial was the way in which Zelma died and the results of the autopsy done by University of Michigan professor Dr. Alfred Scott Warthin. He was able to conduct the autopsy three days after they found the body. Her body had been resting in a coffin at her mother's house, and the doctor asked that it be removed and placed on a table for him to inspect. At first glance, he felt that she had been strangled to death, but his official report was that it was not "violent strangulation." He did notice that there appeared to be fingernail marks on her neck but that her neck didn't have deep bruising, which would have been the result of strangulation and the noose.

Zelma's upper body was pale, but her lower body was almost green in color, and decomposition had quickly set in. This type of discoloration was noted when she was brought down from the tree. Zelma's family doctor, Dr. Warren Maxfield, and Dr. Warthin both stated that this type of discoloration would have taken longer than twenty-four hours to set in, thereby demonstrating that Zelma had been dead for much longer than expected. Her body was extremely low on blood. There were also bruises on her arms that were caused after she had died.

Dr. Warthin noted the smell of asafoetida when he inspected her intestines. Asafoetida was used in abortions. It has a strong odor that is unmistakable, and it has even been nicknamed "devil's dung." It's the extracted gum from an herb and is used in cooking in places like India. Its horrible smell changes as it's cooked. If eaten, some felt that it could induce an abortion. After asafoetida was discovered in her system, there was no doubt in the doctor's mind that Zelma had been dealing with an unwanted pregnancy. As the papers began to speculate on the cause of her death, it came down to three options: poison, smothering or an abortion by an inexperienced hand. Her heart was described as "bloodless," along with other organs, which further suggested the abortion theory. Dr. Warthin strongly felt that Zelma had been given drugs to abort her baby rather than physically going in and removing the fetus and that this is what led to her death. She was buried on October 23, 1913, in Georgetown.

THE TRIAL

On the night Zelma disappeared, the last person to see her alive was a neighbor lady, Mrs. Frieswick. Zelma was returning some dishes that her family had borrowed from Frieswick.

"Morris is waiting for me. I have to go," she told the neighbor, and with that, Zelma let herself out of the house and was never seen alive again. Morris was looking guiltier and guiltier as the trial began. It was proven that her death wasn't from hanging but rather from an abortion gone wrong. So who strung Zelma up in the tree to make it look like it was a suicide? Who wrote the fake notes and left them for her mother to read? Everything was pointing toward Morris, but he wasn't admitting to anything.

The trail progressed slowly as witness after witness was called to the stand to testify what they had seen or what they had known about Zelma's life. Zelma had stayed with her uncle, Robert Cheyne, for some time in Grand Rapids. A bloody handkerchief belonging to Zelma was found in her uncle's barn and brought in for questioning, as was Robert himself. Private investigator C.H. Gravengood had found the same type of knots in Robert's barn as were used in the noose. The defense was trying to get a third party involved to get the guilt off Morris. Robert as a possible suspect didn't hold up well in court, and he was quickly dismissed as the killer. Attorney Smedley had the handkerchief looked at under a microscope, and the red marks were proven to be nothing more than "crimson dirt." Morris's brother, Frank, was dismissed early in the case as well. L.L. Hildreth of Grandville was the undertaker who saw to Zelma's body. According to his testimony, Zelma's uncle Robert told the undertaker to "watch the Atwood boys closely when they viewed the body" when they were at the funeral, as "they were the guilty party."

On February 6, 1914, Morris Atwood finally took the stand, acting on his own behalf. He was described as being "small" and "swarthy." The crowd in the room was ready to hang on to every word the man had to say. Everyone wanted to know why he had been secretly married to Zelma and didn't want to say anything about it to anyone.

Morris said that he had been saving his money so they could start a housekeeping business together. Morris had been living on his father's farm and felt that he didn't have a home to really be able to provide for a wife. He wanted to keep the marriage secret until they could get a place of his own. He didn't want to impose on his father by having Zelma move into the farmhouse with them and just preferred to keep the marriage secret until he could provide a place for them to live. He stated that he hadn't seen Zelma the Saturday she went missing, even though she told her neighbor that she was on her way to meet up with Morris.

Morris never stuttered over his words, nor did his facial expressions change. He was serious and focused as the lawyers came at him with every question they could think of. He was even asked if he had paid for Zelma's funeral, which he said he had done. The prosecution and defense went back and forth with each other until Judge Cross finally told the courtroom that it was time for the jury to make a decision; the lawyers each had one hour apiece to make their pleas.

The jury couldn't agree and argued for hours. At one point, the court started to feel that the jury would never arrive at a verdict until, finally, Judge Cross made them all go to a local hotel and come to a conclusion in the morning. After several hours of deliberation, the jury found Morris Atwood guilty of manslaughter. Given the evidence and how hard the defense fought, many in the courtroom were stunned to hear the verdict. There just wasn't enough evidence to convict Morris of first-degree murder. It was determined that Zelma had an abortion gone wrong and that, rather than come clean about it, Morris decided to make it look like she had killed herself. After sixty days, the case would be moving on to the Supreme Court.

When reporters asked Morris if he was surprised by the verdict, he replied, "Yes, the verdict has surprised me. But I am not the first innocent man to be convicted of a crime." Horace Atwood, Morris's father, was more visibly upset than his son after the verdict was given. Morris's attorney, Charles

Smedley, took the verdict hard as well, seeing as he had known Morris since he was young and considered him part of his family. Smedley stated, "I have been practicing law for twenty nine years and I have had dealings with many criminals. If Atwood is guilty, he is the cleverest criminal I ever saw." Smedley used to work as a schoolteacher in Blendon Township. Horace Atwood was the school director at the time. Smedley used his own past with the Atwood family to try to prove that they were good people and that Morris couldn't possibly be convicted of such a horrible crime.

Atwood pleaded "not guilty" and stuck with his story until the end that he had no idea who killed her or for what reason. The case went to the Supreme Court, but the evidence just seemed stacked against him. If a case like this would have happened in our modern world, forensic science would have solved it in a day, but in 1913, it wasn't that easy to solve. On September 28, 1915, it was announced in the *Grand Haven Tribune* that the Supreme Court upheld the verdict of manslaughter for Morris. Morris wouldn't be walking away a free man anytime soon.

Given the reports, it's hard to believe Atwood wasn't guilty unless there was another, unknown, man involved in the picture. It's possible that Zelma could have gotten herself into a huge mess that only she knew about and that Atwood took the blame being her "secret husband." It was very suspicious that in one of Zelma's supposed notes she stated that Morris isn't "guilty," as if the note was written to try to get all eyes off him and on to some other mystery man in Zelma's life. It seems that the truth went to the grave with poor Zelma Hammond. Morris was out of Jackson by 1930 as the census has him back in Blendon Township. He died on July 10, 1945, at the age of seventy-one.

The Curious Case of Hazel Paine

It's a story for the movies, this story of Hazel Paine. Nothing like it has ever happened in this state. The sensational affair again emphasized the fact that "truth is stranger than fiction."

—Grand Haven Tribune, *December 10, 1913*

Hazel Paine's family had been frantic for months about her condition. They were embarrassed and concerned at the same time, not wanting anyone to find out what they were trying to hide for fear that Hazel's reputation as a good young lady would be ruined. It was January 1913, and Hazel had gone to visit family in nearby Fruitport. In the evening, Hazel and her cousin were walking about the town. She was thirsty and decided to step onto one of the interurban train cars that used to operate and transport people all around Ottawa and neighboring counties in Michigan. Stepping up onto the car, she was greeted by George Clippert, an interurban train dispatcher. She accepted a glass of water, and when she stepped back off the train, she was never quite right after that.

According to Hazel's brother, Orren Paine, from Ferrysburg and her sister, Mabel, living in Spring Lake Township, Hazel told them that she had encountered George Clippert on the train that night and that he had taken advantage of her, leaving her pregnant. In 1913, an unmarried pregnant young girl was kept a secret. So nothing was said to anyone. No doctors were notified to check Hazel out. No neighbors were told of her upcoming motherhood. Everything was kept hidden. As the months went by, the family started to suspect that something strange was happening with Hazel.

Old photograph of the interurban train. *Courtesy of Loutit District Library.*

"Hazel? Are you sure you are pregnant?" they would ask.

"How dare you question me on this!" she'd respond, and in a violent tantrum, Hazel would then leave the house. She had always had a nasty temper. The family could only throw their hands in the air and take her word for it. Why would she lie about such a thing?

As the months blended into summer and the summer welcomed the fall, Hazel's baby was approaching its due date. Mabel Linn contacted Dr. Presley in Grand Haven, letting him know to be at hand because Hazel was soon to have her baby. Andrew Linn, Hazel's brother-in-law, was worried about Hazel. He suspected that she was up to something and became worried when she mentioned going up north to Mears to visit family and that she hoped that when she came back, "everything would be all right." Andrew wondered if Hazel might be thinking of drastic measures with the baby and immediately went to her brother's home and warned Orren not to let her go to Mears, but it was too late. Hazel was nowhere to be found.

BOUND AND TIED UP

It was early evening, and Alfred Wildey, a forty-year-old farmer from Nunica, was walking along the railroad tracks near Crockery Creek on December 2,

1913, on his way for a few groceries. Alfred could hear the Grand Trunk railroad in the far distance making its way eastward and could even see the light of the train visible through the leafless trees. It was a nice fall night, and Alfred wasn't prepared for what was next as his feet collided with something unexpected. He was horrified as he bent down in the darkness to examine what was in his way, holding his lantern in the air to find a young girl stretched across the cold train tracks. Alfred quickly scooped up the nearly lifeless girl and carried her away from the oncoming train that was only minutes away. She was mumbling something and could still walk some.

There was a house nearby, but only men lived there, and Alfred didn't want to bring the barely dressed and battered girl to them. He knew that his wife, Rhoda, and his warm farmhouse in nearby Crockery Township would be a better place, so he partially carried her while she walked the best she could over a mile to his farmhouse. Rhoda was shocked when her husband opened the door with a young woman on his side, looking half dead. Rhoda instantly went to the girl and helped her to an extra bed in the house. The doctor and sheriff were sent for immediately. Tight cords were tied around Hazel's arms, and a corset string was severely tied about her waist. To all who looked at the bindings, it appeared that they were being used to stop circulation and possibly to stop hemorrhaging. The clothes on her were not the ones she was wearing when she left her brother's house on that day, and

Original illustration by Amberrose Hammond.

there were even strips of a man's dress shirt tied around her. The only thing they could get out of her was that she was hungry.

When the girl finally started to come around the next morning, questions came at her from all directions as to how she was found left for dead on the tracks. Sheriff Dykhuis was on the job trying to get to the bottom of the mystery.

"What is your name?" the sheriff asked the girl.

"Hazel Smith. I'm from Shelby," she said weakly.

"Do you have any idea what happened to you or who did this? he asked.

Hazel looked confused and thought for a moment. "I have no idea."

"You have no idea who did this to you? None at all?" pressed the sheriff.

"The last thing I remember is meeting a man at Villa Crossing in Spring Lake. He asked if I would like a buggy ride and I said yes. I sat down next to him and he smiled and offered me a piece of candy. It tasted strange. I don't remember anything after that."

Through the grapevine, Sheriff Dykhuis learned that Hazel had a possible brother and sister living nearby. He made the trek over to Ferrysburg to interview Orren Paine, her brother. Orren was surprised to get a knock on his door from the sheriff.

"Do you have a sister named Hazel Smith?" asked Dykhuis.

"No, but I have one named Hazel Paine," replied Orren. The sheriff figured that she said her last name was Smith because she was still mentally confused and injured.

Orren told the sheriff everything about Hazel he could think of. She had been pregnant and was soon to deliver. They had kept everything hidden because they didn't want Hazel to be shamed for what had happened. But the strangest thing in the whole story was that Hazel wasn't pregnant anymore. What had become of the baby? And who had been the father?

Orren said that Hazel had always spoken about a George Clippert, a train dispatcher for the interurban. He mentioned a time when they were getting onto the interurban and George was operating—Hazel became frozen in fear. The family had even gone as far as to approach George about the situation. They claimed that they had visited him, writing him a letter explaining everything that Hazel had told them. They asked for $100 to help with delivery costs. George told them that it was blackmail, that he had no idea who Hazel was and that they had the wrong man. And that was that. George shut the door, and the family figured that they were on their own with this one. After George Clippert's name was brought up, the sheriff had no other option than to send some men to his house and bring him to the jail for questioning.

As soon as possible, police went to George's house in Fruitport and arrested him. His wife was furious, and George kept saying that he had no idea who this Hazel Paine girl was. George had a nice family between his wife and baby, and they felt shame that they were getting dragged into this awful situation. George only sat in jail for a couple of days before he was released on the basis that there just wasn't enough evidence to convict him. His boss wrote a solid letter as to his character, and he was able to provide a sturdy alibi as to his whereabouts on the night Hazel was discovered. He admitted that he recognized the girl from riding the interurban and did mention that the family had tried to get money out of him. George told them, "This is blackmail and we will not be a part of this!"

With Clippert out of jail and back home, Deputy Sheriff Wildey still strongly felt that there had been an attempted murder, but all he had to go with evidence-wise was the mysterious set of men's tracks next to Hazel's footprints found by the railroad tracks. Given the low-tech crime scene investigation techniques they had in 1913, the tracks could have belonged to anyone, even Alfred.

Something Just Isn't Right with Hazel

The local physician, Dr. White from Nunica, made his way out to Crockery Township to examine Hazel. The family didn't want to move her just yet, feeling that she was fragile, and Mrs. Wildey was okay with watching over the girl. Mrs. Wildey reported that Hazel would sleep well all night but then wake up in the morning and just stare at nothing as if she were in a trance, her body stiff and rigid. She would fall asleep during the day occasionally and in her sleep blurt out, "My baby! My baby!" and "Don't let him take me again!" Hazel seemed to say a lot of things in her sleep, as her sister-in-law remembered Hazel telling her everything that had happened to her, supposedly involving George Clippert, while she was "asleep." During some of her delusions, she would ramble off names of local men.

Dr. White and a few other physicians who had looked at Hazel all noticed that there were no signs of pregnancy, and there certainly didn't seem to be signs of a "criminal operation" or abortion—or even a live birth for that matter. Judging by the time she had admitted that George Clippert supposedly abused her, Hazel's baby was overdue by a month. The cops were having a very difficult time finding anyone to blame for this, and people were starting to question if Hazel was "right in the head." She looked much older than seventeen, was considered very pretty and by no means appeared "insane," as the newspapers reported, but something wasn't right.

Orren believed that Hazel was "obstinately holding something back" and was playing dumb on purpose, acting as if she couldn't remember anything. Whenever Hazel was asked something by her family or the police, she acted as if she were too weak to talk or tried to act confused. She claimed that her memory was fuzzy on all accounts as to what happened that night. Everyone was suspicious of what Hazel was up to. If this was all a dangerous act she was putting on, what purpose did it serve? What was Hazel hiding? The family eventually moved her back to Spring Lake. The reporters and local people swarmed the Wildey farm in the hopes of catching a glimpse of this now notorious local girl. Newspapers from out of state had even reported on the mysterious situation surrounding Hazel. But her brother and sister kept her covered, got her in a wagon and arranged a private interurban train to get her back home.

After Hazel was moved from the Wildey farmhouse in Crockery Township, Mrs. Wildey discovered a baby dress and a motor hood under the mattress on which Hazel had been sleeping. They were Hazel's, who said that she had gotten rid of those two articles of clothing a year earlier. Hazel claimed that she had no idea how they got there, and Mrs. Wildey turned them over to the police. The whole story just kept getting more and more confusing by the day.

As police continued to search for clues without any luck, Prosecutor Osterhouse felt that it was totally possible for Hazel to have tied the bands around herself with no problem. Dr. White also agreed that Hazel could have tied the cords herself as the knots around her waist and arms were tied in the front, not the back. The doctor said that tying a cord about the waist would never stop a hemorrhage and that it "would have no effect whatsoever." It appeared that all of the cords were attempts to cut off blood flow, but for what reason? It was decided that she had never been pregnant. Hazel had been obviously lying about it, and some were even considering her insane, saying that she made up the sexual assault and the pregnancy and that neither had happened.

The real mystery was who brought Hazel to the train tracks and made it look like she had been left for dead. There was no doubt to the police that she had help in the situation. All of the interurban conductors knew Hazel, and none of them could say that they saw her the afternoon she disappeared. She had been spotted around Spring Lake about 3:00 p.m., when she got onto the interurban. Some even believed that the relatives themselves were hiding something. As the *Grand Haven Tribune* wrote, "It is not beyond reason to believe that she is entirely the victim of her own insane imagination." Dr. White started to believe that the girl was naturally "hysterical" and that she had never been drugged by anyone the night she was found.

Hazel's cousin even said that George Clippert was not "responsible for Hazel's condition." She went on to say that "Hazel and I were near the warehouse after dark that night. Hazel wanted a drink and went inside the car with Clippert to get it. They were not gone a minute. I am sure that nothing happened then."

The courts wanted to see Hazel get a full mental examination, and Dr. Fuller out of Grand Rapids was contacted to evaluate her. A local physician, Dr. DeKleine, also stated that Hazel's story was a total "myth" after examining her on December 6, 1913. On Wednesday, December 10, Hazel was brought into the Ottawa County jail for questioning. The police were fed up and wanted answers straight from the source. This was a waste of their time and resources for what was appearing to be a strange prank.

Sheriff Dykhuis wasn't entirely ready to give up yet. The possibility of murder still sat in the shadows, and after talking to some people in Grand Rapids, he felt that he was on to something again but wouldn't divulge any information until he knew for certain. But nothing ever came of it.

There was no convincing Alfred that Hazel had made everything up and did this to herself. Alfred even stated "on two different nights since the occurrence, men have been skulking about near his farm," since Hazel had been staying there. His dogs woke him up one night barking wildly. Alfred looked out his window and saw two men walking away from his farm.

On about December 20, Hazel was eventually released from the jail, and she went back home in Oceana County up north and wasn't really ever heard from again.

It can probably be assumed that Hazel was the victim of "false pregnancy" (or its medical term, pseudocyesis). It's very rare and typically starts in the mind. The body goes through all of the motions as if it were pregnant. This could have been what kept her family believing that she was going to have a baby. Or they just simply took her word for it and she kept pillows stuffed under her dress. It's possible that she also suffered from an undiagnosed mental disorder as well, seeing that many problems like that went undiscovered or just caused people to end up in an asylum. The police were never able to get anything out of her, and the case was closed.

The *Grand Haven Tribune* reported, "In Nunica one can hear a number of ugly rumors in connection with the affair it is stated and there are a number of people there who have settled convictions, but when it comes to pinning them down and getting absolute facts, it is impossible and the Hazel Paine mystery is liable to be a mystery forever and may furnish gossip for many years to come."

The Wilson Pound Murder

This was one of the most cold blooded and atrocious in Michigan criminal annals.
—Grand Rapids Press, *July 11, 1903*

Old Wilson Pound was a bit of a hermit. He was unmarried and had a small cabin that overlooked Black Lake in Holland. He lived a peaceful existence fishing and trapping small animals. Rumor had it that Wilson Pound was rich and had thousands of dollars buried on his property. Michigan has seen its fair share of horrible crimes since its creation, but in 1875, when Wilson Pound was discovered murdered, it was considered one of the worst and most gruesome in the state's early years.

According to John S. Watson, on July 5, 1875, John H. Fuller asked him if he wanted to go fishing with him and his son, Melvin. John thought it sounded like fun and agreed to meet the two men. Fuller told Watson they would be picking up Wilson Pound to go fishing with them as well. By all accounts, it sounded like it was going to be a nice day fishing with "the boys" at Pine Creek Bay. Fuller asked Watson if he minded picking Pound up with his horse cart. Watson said he would and went to pick up the old bachelor.

Once at Pine Creek, the men set up their gear and got to fishing. Melvin had secured a small rowboat to take out in the water. The men fished all day. Pound went in the boat with Melvin and came back again. All of them had a good time casting their lines off the docks. As the sun started to set, John Fuller asked Pound if he wanted to go out in the boat again. Pound said he would, and they invited Watson to come out with them. "No…three is enough men for that small boat. I'll stay here," said Watson. He watched John Fuller put an axe and a long spear in the boat with them and row off into the lake and out of sight.

When Watson noticed the boat coming back into view, he could only see two men. John Fuller and his son, Melvin, rowed the boat up to the shore and got out. Watson was confused and asked, "Where's Pound at?"

John Fuller looked Watson in the eyes and stated, "We got Pound right where we want him and if you ever lisp a word about this, I'll shoot you." Watson knew something bad had been done to poor Pound. The men started to empty the rowboat. Watson noticed that the long spear was missing.

John Fuller said that he had killed Pound because he was the principal witness in a suit pending against him. Pound had witnessed John Fuller tearing up a railroad track. Fuller kept saying things like, "but I had to do it or go to Jackson [prison]." Watson asked Fuller if he got anything from Pound, and Fuller replied, "Yes, I got enough to pay for my trouble." John may have tried to threaten Pound in exchange for some of his wealth and to keep him quiet about the lawsuit, but in the end, he just decided that Pound was better off silenced by the grave. John and Melvin continued to bully Watson, showing him weapons and saying that it would be the end of his life if he ever spoke about what had happened that day. According to the *Jackson Daily Citizen*, Fuller offered Watson ten dollars and potentially forty acres if he would keep quiet.

When other neighbors and townsfolk noticed that Pound hadn't been seen in a week at any of his usual haunts, they started to suspect that he might be haunting another area, one not of this world. Police smelled foul play in the air, and a search party was immediately formed in the hopes of finding the man. Suspicion was quickly cast on the neighbors, John Fuller, Melvin and John Watson. John Watson was the first arrest made, and the first chance he got, he told police that he was with the men the night of the murder but that it had been committed by John Fuller and his son.

Watson was with the police when Pound's body was found near a little cave at the mouth of the Pine Creek. The body was naked and had been struck on the head with an axe, disemboweled and strapped to a tall metal spear. The murderous father and son had hoped by strapping Pound to the long spear and taking out his insides that he would stay at the bottom of the water forever and never come back to haunt them. As the men were first searching the water, prosecuting attorney Mr. Adsit, who was on the boat with Watson and the police, noticed a large number of flies on the water.

Adsit grabbed a boat hook, moved the weeds and plants off the water and uncovered the bloated, decaying body of Wilson Pound. Watson said that he "was an unwilling participant" and was the first to take the stand when the trial began.

Old man Fuller confessed and was sent to Jackson Prison for a life sentence. John Fuller took all of the blame but continued to say Watson was a "willing accessory." Watson's testimony that he wasn't a witness to the actual murder was helped by a group of men from Barry County. They were fishing on the lake that evening when they noticed a skiff go by their cabin with three men in the boat.

The son, Melvin, was acquitted of the crime after a twelve-hour deliberation from the jury because the father took the full blame. Old man Fuller was sent to Jackson and escaped from the prison a few years later, never to be found again. A rumor from a 1903 *Grand Rapids Press* article had it that Fuller had recently died in California. Watson left the United States after the trial.

Bank Robbers and Mobsters

Bank robbers are the aristocracy of the criminal profession.
–Eddie Bentz

The People's Savings Bank was on the corner of Third and Washington Streets in the downtown area of Grand Haven. Little did the poor employees of the bank know that their place was being scoped out for a big robbery. This would be a quick and easy job for Eddie Bentz and his boys. They would be in and out of there in no time with some nice cash. Eddie knew what he was good at, and it was bank robbing.

Edward Wilhelm Bentz had dabbled in crime his whole life, sending him in and out of juvenile detention facilities. His troubled youth led to more ambitious crimes and eventually to bank robbing in the 1930s, stealing millions of dollars from banks across the United States.

Eddie used his farm boy charm and easygoing demeanor to talk to people in the bank to get an idea about the employees and the security in the building before he would rob the place. He spent time in public libraries learning about the banking system to come up with a formula to estimate how much money a particular bank would possibly have in its safe at a given time. By all means, he was an intelligent criminal. When he wasn't robbing banks, he preferred to live a quiet life collecting rare books. He claimed to have robbed more than one hundred banks in his lifetime and was never caught in some huge robberies, such as a $2 million job in Lincoln, Nebraska, in 1930.

On September 29, 1932, Eddie and his gang were already lurking around quiet little Ottawa County. Their target was the First State Bank in Holland. Early in the morning, Eddie and his boys burst into the bank through the front doors. The bank tellers and early morning customers screamed as the men raised their guns and yelled the classic line, "This is a holdup!" The people panicked as they were forced to get down on the ground, putting their faces against the cold, hard floor. They demanded to know who the cashier was and who knew how to open the bank vault.

Thanks to a few people hearing the commotion from outside and one poor soul who walked in and ran right back out screaming that the bank was being robbed, the cops were quickly alerted. When Chief Lievense walked up to the bank's front door, the robbers drew their guns and started shooting, sending the officer down with a bullet. The chief was able to get up and run for more backup. As the bandits made for their getaway cars, more gunfire rained down on the town.

To help take out the cop cars following them, the gang spread nails all over the roads. They made off with more than $12,000. Only two men were badly wounded by the gunfire that morning, but thankfully they lived. Feeling like he had enough money to live off of, and perhaps worrying that his luck was soon to run out, Eddie retreated from bank robbing after the Holland robbery and moved to Long Beach, Indiana.

Eddie was considering retiring from bank robbing altogether in 1931. The thirty-six-year-old Bentz had married a young girl of only eighteen and was looking to settle down. He had enough money stashed away and planned on being a consultant to other bank robbers for a fee.

In 1933, the five-foot-four, twenty-five-year-old Lester Gillis, better known as Baby Face Nelson, approached Eddie for advice on a good bank to rob. He invited Bentz to join his gang for a few more robberies. Eddie couldn't resist. Bank robbing was in his blood. He suggested Grand Haven, Michigan, and the People's Savings Bank and got to work researching the building and planning for another perfect robbery.

The mug shot of Lester Gillis, aka Baby Face Nelson. *Courtesy of Library of Congress.*

Baby Face Nelson got his criminal start early in his life, just like Eddie had. By his early twenties, he was stealing jewelry from millionaire homes and getting involved with some big-time criminals around Chicago. He earned his nickname due to the fact that he looked really young and was very short. Baby Face would ultimately become notorious as Public Enemy No. 1 when he became involved in the John Dillinger murder in Chicago. Five months after John Dillinger died, the Federal Bureau of Investigation (FBI) found Baby Face, and he was killed during a gunfight with agents in Chicago. His gig with Eddie Bentz would be his first big bank heist and would inspire him to rob more banks.

EVERYTHING GOES WRONG

On August 18, 1933, the little town of Grand Haven wasn't ready for the excitement that would hit when Eddie Bentz and four other robbers came to town. Two well-dressed men, short in stature, stepped into the bank just before 3:00 p.m. One man walked up to a teller and pushed a ten-dollar bill over. "I'd like two dollars in nickels and two dollars in dimes please."

"Certainly Sir," said bank teller Arthur Welling, and he turned around to go get the change. Call it intuition, but something made Arthur take a second look at the two men. As he was getting the change, he noticed the other well-dressed man walk toward the back of the lobby. A feeling of dread came over Arthur, and something inside told him that these men were bank robbers. Arthur's heart was racing, but he walked back toward the man at the window and started to count his change back to him. Arthur's suspicions were correct when the man across from him lifted a gun to his face.

"Keep still," said the man. Arthur immediately stepped on the bank's silent alarm below the window that went straight to the police and even alerted Edward Kinkema in the furniture store next to the bank. The bandits had no idea what was about to happen to them in a short time.

Meanwhile, the gang of men forced everyone in the bank to lie down on the floor while the men emptied the cash tills at each window. One of the bandits walked up to the group of terrified people lying on the floor.

"Where is the cashier!?" he yelled at them.

Poor F.C. Bolt slowly responded in fear. "I am," he said.

"Open the vault!" yelled the man at Bolt. The scared man attempted to open the huge door but had to admit that he wasn't used to opening the door and didn't really know how to do it.

The People's Savings Bank. *Courtesy of Loutit District Library.*

"Well who can open it then?" the man demanded.

Poor Arthur Welling admitted that he could do it and was escorted to the vault with a gun poking into his ribs. Arthur knew that the police were on their way, so he tried to move the numbers on the combination as slowly as possible, but the gunman behind him caught on quickly and threatened to shoot if he didn't make it quick. The click of the dial falling into the open position was heard by the robber, and he yelled, "Pull open the door!"

Arthur pulled the heavy door open, and the men rushed into the vault, grabbing everything they could get their greedy hands on. After the money was gathered, the gang looked at the people lying on the floor. The men knew without a doubt that citizens were aware of what was going on inside the bank. Their time was running short if they wanted to make a clean getaway.

"Do we take just the girls out with us?" one man asked the gang. "Or do we just bring them all out in front of us?" If the men used the bank employees as human shields, no one would be shooting at them as they got into the getaway car that was waiting for them outside. Eddie Bentz started to feel that this robbery was a bust but was confident that they would get out of it. What the men didn't realize was that their getaway car had already driven away. Hero of the day Edward Kinkema noticed the suspicious driver sitting in a black Buick. When the driver saw Edward walking with his shotgun, he quickly drove off rather than be shot at. Forget the gang! They were doomed on this one. He was going to protect himself while he still could. It was said that the driver's name was Freddie, and after he made his way back to Chicago after fleeing the scene, he was killed three days later.

When the men exited the back of the building with the employees as human shields around them, they heard the police enter the front of the bank. The men looked around outside for the black car, but there was none to be seen.

"Where the hell is the car!?" yelled Baby Face Nelson. Panic started to settle in the bottom of the robbers' stomachs. The situation had turned very ugly.

Needing to keep the police at bay, the bandits fired off their machine guns, spraying bullets everywhere. Three of the robbers headed behind the bank to nearby Franklin Street in search of a car. They forced a car with two women and four children inside to pull over. At first, the bandits debated if they should keep the children with them for added protection against being fired at, but after seeing the mother's panic, the men must have had a soft spot in one brief moment and let the children out of the Chevrolet sedan. The men drove off and headed toward their freedom on highway U.S. 31 southbound and onward to Indiana.

As the bandits made off with some of the money, but not all, heavily armed police began setting up barricades throughout the county hoping to catch the men but gave up hope after the getaway car was found in West Olive. The men had held up another unsuspecting car owner and taken off in a different car to help them escape the state lines. Once the men escaped into Indiana, the Michigan police couldn't follow them anymore, and the men were free.

One of the six gang members, Earl Doyle, was the only man captured by the police. He was found holding a gun to Bolt's chest when Kinkema used the butt of his gun on the bandit's head and sent the man to the floor. Once on the floor, locals were able to grab the man and secure him so that he wouldn't be a threat anymore. While sitting in the Ottawa County jail with injuries and a fractured leg, Earl wouldn't speak a word to anyone about the other members of the gang.

In the end, the bank stated that the total amount taken was only $2,500 and that it would be covered by insurance. Initially, the amount was more than $20,000, but most of the stolen loot had been left behind in the abandoned Chrysler in West Olive. According to local historian David Seibold, "the final bank accounting showed a loss of 2,568 in cash, 6,410 in bank checks and seven railroad bonds."

Thankfully, only four citizens were wounded among the chaos of the machine gun bullets. Peter Van Loplik was hit in the neck and arm, and he was taken to the hospital. Captain Julius Pleines was in the hospital with a back wound and had the worst injury. John Lindemulder, a bank cashier, was grazed by a bullet on his back. William Pellegrom, a bank teller, was shot in the foot. Funny enough, the bank's cleaner, Leoria VanDyke, had been hiding in the broom closet the entire time, listening to the whole event play out while trying not to make a sound.

Eventually, Eddie Bentz was put on the FBI's most wanted list after bank robbing became a federal crime. He and his wife, Verna, tried to go into hiding. Young Verna decided that laying low with her criminal husband wasn't the life for her, and she left him. When Verna went back home to Milwaukee, she was immediately questioned by FBI as to the whereabouts of her ex-husband. The endless questions finally released a place in New York, where they eventually found Bentz hiding out in 1936 and arrested him. His first big prison trip was to Alcatraz, where he stayed until 1948. But Eddie just couldn't keep his hand out of the candy jar and was put in prison numerous times after that up through 1962. That year he finally managed to stay out of jail. He died on October 31, 1979, at the age of eighty-five.

Eddie did end up confessing to the Grand Haven robbery and to the other men involved: Tommy Carroll, Lester "Baby Face Nelson" Gillis, Earl Doyle and Chuck Fisher. Supposedly, Bentz told FBI agents that he had buried $20,000 in bonds and traveler's checks from the People's Savings robbery in southwest Michigan. The FBI claimed that it never found anything. Rumors were passed around of hidden money being found in Grand Haven for which the robbers were going to come back someday. It's an incredible piece of mobster history and leaves many residents in Grand Haven and Holland talking about it to this day.

Conclusion

When All Hope Is Lost

As I pored through endless hours of newspapers, I couldn't help but start to chuckle about how blunt they were in regards to reporting on suicides and everything in general. The stories in this book are sad, sometimes poignant, often gross and ever so often worth a laugh, as in the case of Thomas Mahan. I've collected interesting obituaries from the *Coopersville Observer*, and I'll leave you with some of the most shocking reports that no one would see in modern papers today.

"Blendon Man Kills Himself With Gun: Careful in Arranging House Previous to Shooting" was the title of an October 7, 1927 article from the *Coopersville Observer*. Louis De Jonge lived in a farmhouse and operated a poultry farm in Blendon Township. His sister had died about a year and a half ago, and her husband recently went to the Kalamazoo State Hospital—or asylum, as it was usually called. The unmarried Louis would soon be in charge of six small children after the farm his sister and brother-in-law had owned was auctioned off.

On the morning of October 5, Louis arose from sleep and prepared for his last day on earth. He neatly placed his best Sunday clothes on his dining room table. He put all of his important papers, valuables and what money he had in one place, and then he headed outside to his front porch. Sitting down for the last time, he picked up his double-barreled shotgun and propped it so the butt of the gun rested on the windowsill behind him and the barrel of the gun met up with his head; then he pulled the trigger.

Eventually, a little ten-year-old neighbor boy came walking past the farmhouse. He saw Louis sitting on his porch but wasn't prepared for the gruesome sight that was in front of him. The newspaper reported that "a man was sitting on the porch without any head." Perhaps poor Louis, not knowing how he was going to emotionally and financially handle six children, all of a sudden decided that suicide was his only option.

When readers of the *Coopersville Observer* picked up their daily paper on March 23, 1928, they got to read that "Mrs. Elizabeth Steiner, 63 years old, was found by her husband hung from the bedroom door of their home in Conklin." They had moved from Port Huron, and the husband figured that it had just been "too much for her."

On October 2, 1908, it was reported that "George Lawton Takes Poison and Cuts His Throat. He was very despondent." George had experienced a poor crop, and his wife's health had been bad for years. He decided to take a bunch of morphine and some "paris green" and then slit his throat in case the other two didn't work. Paris green was a highly toxic substance that was used in pigments and gained its name as a rat killer in Paris. At one point, it was even used as a pesticide on apples in the United States in about 1900.

There are newspaper articles that make anyone raise an eyebrow, such as this title from 1919 from Crockery township: "Child Caught on Rail Guard Killed by Car: Motorman Thought Body was a Newspaper." Now who mistakes a body for a newspaper?

If the family of Zelma Hammond, from the chapter "She Was Found Swinging in the Wind," hadn't experienced enough tragedy with the murder of their daughter, the *Grand Haven Tribune* reported that the "sister-in-law of Zelma Hammond, kills self at home in Hudsonville." The article is from December 9, 1914, just a year after Zelma had been killed. Her sister claimed that she was "tired of living" and asked her family in a note to take care of her children. She swallowed carbolic acid.

Our modern world seems to have violence around every corner, but the days of the past had just as much danger and tragedy, even in Ottawa County. I hope you enjoyed reading these twisted tales from the past as much as I enjoyed digging them up.

Bibliography

The Brutal Murder of Enos Lawrence

Grand Haven Tribune. "Circuit Court." Friday, August 14, 1896.
———. "Circuit Court." Monday, August 17, 1896.
———. "Circuit Court." Saturday, August 15, 1896.
———. "Circuit Court." Thursday, August 13, 1896.
———. "Circuit Court." Tuesday, August 11, 1896.
———. "Circuit Court." Wednesday, August 12, 1896.
———. "Dr. Wetmore Bound Over." Thursday, September 17, 1896.
———. "A Full Confession." Monday, April 27, 1896.
———. "Jackson for Life." Wednesday, August 19, 1896.
———. "The Murder Case." Tuesday, September 15, 1896.
———. "Wetmore's Examination." Wednesday, September 16, 1896.
———. "Wetmore in Jail." Monday, September 14, 1896.
———. "Twenty Years in Prison." Saturday, September 19, 1896.
Grand Rapids Press. "Bad Trio." Monday, September 14, 1896.
———. "Dr. Wetmore Again." Saturday, September 10, 1904.
———. "Will Plead Insanity." Wednesday, August 12, 1896
Jackson Citizen. "Dr. Wetmore Free." Friday, November 13, 1896.
———. "The Holland Murder." Friday, April 24, 1896.
———. "The Holland Murder." Friday, May 1, 1896.
———. "She Is a Degenerate." Tuesday, December 1, 1896.

Kalamazoo Gazette. "Big Mob." Friday, May 1, 1896.

———. "The Wife Arrested." Wednesday, April 22, 1896.

Muskegon Chronicle. "That Holland Murder Case." Friday, April 24, 1896.

———. "The Holland Murder Mystery." Thursday, April 23, 1896.

———. "The Holland Murder Mystery." Wednesday, April 22, 1896.

———. "In Second Degree." Thursday, September 3, 1896.

———. "She Seeks a Pardon." Friday, June 18, 1897.

Ottawa County Times. "An Awful Crime." Friday, May 1, 1896.

———. "A Confession."Friday, April 24, 1896.

———. "Guilty, Murder in the First Degree. Friday, August 21, 1896.

If He Can't Have Her, No One Will

Coopersville Observer. "Egbert 'Happy' Dyke Slays Marne Teacher." Friday, October 24, 1924.

———. "Happy Dyke Given 15 Years in Jackson." Friday, December 12, 1924.

Grand Haven Tribune. "Dyke Tells Story of Tragic Day in Murder Trial." Friday, November 21, 1924.

———. "Final Curtain of Tragic Drama Is Raised in Court." Thursday, November 20, 1924.

———. "Happy Dyke Cleaned Up and Shaved." Tuesday, October 21, 1924.

———. "Happy Dyke Is Happy in County Jail." Monday, November 24, 1924.

———. "Happy Dyke Talks Little of His Case." Wednesday, October 22, 1924.

———. "Happy Dyke to Face Trial for Killing Teacher." Wednesday, November 19, 1924.

———. "Happy Dyke Wins Lesser Verdict in Murder Case." Saturday, November 22, 1924.

———. "Jilted Lover Slays School Teacher." Saturday, October 18, 1924.

———. "Large Crowd at Court for Examination." Tuesday, October 28, 1924.

———. "Slayer Awaits Fate in County Jail." Monday, October 20, 1924.

The Ku Klux Klan in Ottawa County

Bartoletti, Susan Campbell. *They Called Themselves the K.K.K.* Boston: Houghton Mifflin, 2010.

Enders, Calvin W. "Under Grand Haven's White Sheets." *Michigan Historical Review* 19, no. 1 (1993): 49–61.

———. "White Sheets in Mecosta: The Anatomy of a Michigan Klan." *Michigan Historical Review* 14, no. 1 (1988): 59–84.

Fox, Craig. *Everyday Klansfolk: White Protestant Life and the KKK in 1920s Michigan.* East Lansing: Michigan State University Press, 2011.

Grand Haven Tribune. "Appearance of Ku Klux in City Causes Much Talk of Klan and Organization." Tuesday, September 18, 1923.

———. "Burning Crosses on Dewey Hill Believed to Have Had Start at Hands of Kid Klan." Tuesday, September 25, 1923.

———. "Holland Paper Hands Big Slam at Ku Klux Klan When Printed Letter Is Sent." October 2, 1923.

———. "Ku Klux Klan Evidence Is Now Unearthed." Saturday, August 25, 1923.

———. "Ku Klux Klan Is Working in Holland City." Tuesday, August 21, 1923.

———. "Rumor of Klan Meeting Here Last Night Causes Conjecture on All Sides." Wednesday, September 26, 1923.

Newton, Michael. *The Ku Klux Klan.* Jefferson, NC: Mcfarland & Company, 2007.

THE NOTORIOUS BOSTON BLACKIE

Grand Haven Tribune. "Daily Tribune." April 5, 1900.

———. "Daily Tribune." April 14, 1900.

———. "Daily Tribune." April 9, 1900.

———. "Daily Tribune." April 17, 1900.

———. "Daily Tribune." April 6, 1900.

———. "Daily Tribune." April 12, 1900.

———. "Daily Tribune." Saturday, March 31, 1900.

———. "Daily Tribune." Tuesday, April 3, 1900.

———. "Daily Tribune." Wednesday, April 4, 1900.

———. "A Saloon Shooting." Wednesday, March 28, 1900.

———. "That Shooting Affair." Thursday, March 29, 1900.

GOODBYE GRANDMA!

Bay City Times. "Commutation of Sentence." Wednesday, April 24, 1901.

Grand Haven Tribune. "Cheesbro Confesses." Wednesday, July 10, 1895.

———. "Daily Evening Tribune." Friday, July 12, 1895.
———. "Daily Evening Tribune." Monday, July 15, 1895.
———. "Daily Evening Tribune." Thursday, July 11, 1895.
———. "Daily Evening Tribune." Tuesday, July 23, 1895.
———. "Daily Evening Tribune." Wednesday, July 10, 1895.
———. "Funeral of Mrs. Levi Pierce." Thursday, July 11, 1895.
———. "Murder at Tallmadge." Tuesday, July 9, 1895.
Grand Rapids Press. "Avenged the Girl." Wednesday, July 10, 1895.
———. "To Prison for Life." Friday, August 16, 1895.
Jackson Citizen. "Boy Now Dead." Tuesday, June 4, 1901.
Muskegon Chronicle. "The Defendant on the Witness Stand." Friday, September 6, 1895.

The Fury of a Lynch Mob

Barnett, LeRoy. "Lynch Law in Michigan." *Chronicle: The Historical Society of Michigan* 28, no. 1 (2005): 10–13.
Holland City News. "When Holland Nearly Had a Lynching Bee." Thursday, September 9, 1909.
Stonehouse, Frederick. *Great Lakes Crime II.* Gwinn, MI: Avery Color Studios, 2007.

The Heartache of Daniel Hawkins

Grand Haven Tribune. "Daily Evening Tribune." Wednesday, January 31, 1894.
———. "Tragedy in Robinson." Monday, January 29, 1894.
———. "Verdict of Suicide." Tuesday, January 30, 1894.

Argument Over Cows Ends in Death

Coopersville Observer. "Was Determined to Die." Friday, October 2, 1908.
———. "Woman Is Slain." Friday, November 26, 1909.
Grand Haven Tribune. "Attempt to Prove Seelman a Mad Man." Friday, January, 21, 1910.
———. "Daily Tribune." Friday, October 18, 1901
———. "Daily Tribune." Monday, October 14, 1901.

———. "Daily Tribune." Saturday, October 12, 1901
———. "Daily Tribune." Wednesday, October 16, 1901
———. "Death Stalked Chester." Monday, November 22, 1909.
———. "Edna Faylor Visits Seelman." Tuesday, November 23, 1909.
———. "Experts in Seelman Case." Saturday, January, 22, 1910.
———. "Murder Case." Thursday, January, 20, 1910.
———. "Murderer Is Arraigned." Tuesday, November 23, 1909.
———. "Seelman Case Is Over." Tuesday, January, 25, 1910.
———. "Seelman Sentenced Today." Thursday, January, 27, 1910.
———. "Verdict in Lesser Degree." Friday, January, 28, 1910.
Grand Rapids Press. "Behind a Horse Farmer Found With a Crushed Skull." Monday, October 14, 1901.

MAGICAL, MAGNETIC WATER! AND FAKE CURES AND PESTILENCE

Anderson, Ann. *Snake Oil, Hustlers and Hambones*. Jefferson, NC: McFarland & Company, 2000.
Carson, Gerald. *One For a Man, Two For a Horse*. New York: Bramhall House, 1961.
Dryfhout, John H. "The Saratoga of the West." *Inland Seas* 20, no. 3 (1964): 185–95.
Ewing, Wallace K., PhD. *Directory of Buildings & Sites in Northwest Ottawa County*. Grand Haven, MI: Tri-Cities Historical Museum, 2008.
Grand Haven Tribune. "Shield Family." Friday, September 28, 1894.
———. "Shield Family." Monday, October 1, 1894.
———. "Shield Family." Thursday, September 27, 1894.
———. "Shield Family." Tuesday, October 2, 1894.
———. "Shield Family." Wednesday, September 26, 1894.
Hodgson, Barbara. *In the Arms of Morpheus: The Tragic History of Laudanum, Morphine, and Patent Medicine*. New York: Firefly Books, 2001.
Holbrook, Stewart H. *The Golden Age of Quackery*. New York: Macmillian Company, 1959.
Rayner & Buck. *Magnetic Spring Water*. Chicago: Lakeside Press, 1870.
Seibold, David H. *Grand Haven: In the Path of Destiny*. Grand Haven, MI: D-2 Enterprises, 2008.

The Wrath of a Husband

Coopersville Observer. "Fred B. Allison. Former Athlete, Dies at Nunica." Thursday, May 1, 1952.

Grand Haven Tribune. "Allison Improves Hopes for Recovery." Thursday, April 16, 1914.

———. "Attorneys Refuse to Answer Questions." Thursday, August 5, 1915.

———. "Capt. Thomas Mahon Dies at Age of 96." Monday, May 26, 1969.

———. "Children to Live in Sight of Father's Prison." Wednesday, August 11, 1915.

———. "Court Room Stirred by Real Life's Drama." Saturday, August 7, 1915.

———. "Examination Not Set; Two Cases in Court." Wednesday, December 30, 1914.

———. "Judge Cross Orders Verdict of Not Guilty in Dykhuis Case." Thursday, August 5, 1915.

———. "Judge Waits on Mahon to Receive Sentence." Monday, December 7, 1914.

———. "Mahon Back to Jail in Default of Bond." Saturday, April 18, 1914.

———. "Mahon Case Begins; Expect Insanity Plea." Monday, November 23, 1914.

———. "Mahon Smiles When Verdict of Guilty Is Returned." Wednesday, November 25, 1914.

———. "Mahon to Ionia 1 to 10 Years." Monday, December 28, 1914.

———. "Mrs. Leona Mahon Testifies in Exam." Thursday, January 7, 1915.

———. "Mrs. Mahon's Recital Bares Whole Scandal." Tuesday, November 24, 1914.

———. "Mrs. Thomas Mahon Is Sentenced Today." Tuesday, August 10, 1915.

———. "Petition for Pardon of 'Turk' Allison." Tuesday, October 5, 1915.

———. "Sees Wife with Another; Man Commits Heinous Assault." Wednesday, April 15, 1914.

———. "Sensational Case Adjourned to 14th." Friday, January 8, 1915.

———. "Seven Are Sentenced Before Judge Cross." Wednesday, September 29, 2915.

———. "Sheriff Bound Over; Requests Trial Soon." Thursday, January 14, 1915.

———. "Sheriff Helps Draw Own Jury for Trial." Saturday, February 20, 1915.

———. "State Pardon Board Look Up Mahon Case." Friday, August 13, 1915.
———. "Thomas Mahon Has Been Paroled by Gov." Thursday, August 19, 1915.
———. "Victim of Assault Tells Own Story." Friday, April 17, 1914.

SHE WAS FOUND SWINGING IN THE WIND

Coopersville Observer. "Woman's Body Hanging from Tree." Friday, October 31, 1913.
Grand Haven Tribune. "Attorney Smedley Cross Examines Robert Cheyne." February 5, 1914.
———. "Atwood Boys Are Arrested." Wednesday, October 29, 1913.
———. "Atwood Case Again Postponed." Saturday, November 29, 1913.
———. "Atwood Case Progressing." Tuesday, February 3, 1914.
———. "Atwood Examination in Justice Court." Tuesday, December 9, 1913.
———. "Atwood Examination Is Now On." Monday, December 8, 1913.
———. "Atwood Examination Resumed Monday." Monday, December 22, 1913.
———. "Atwoods Arraigned in Justice Court." Saturday, November 8, 1913.
———. "Atwood's Furnish Heavy Bail." Tuesday, December 23, 1913.
———. "Atwood's Will Take the Witness Stand." Wednesday, February 4, 1914.
———. "Jury Finds Morris Atwood Guilty." February 7, 1914.
———. "Morris Atwood Testifies in His Own Behalf." February 5, 1914.
———. "Mystery in Death of Hanging Woman." Monday, October 27, 1913.
———. "Woman's Body Swinging in the Wind." Saturday, October 25, 1913.
Grand Rapids Press. "Ottawa Woman May Be Murder Victim." Saturday, October 25, 1913.

THE CURIOUS CASE OF HAZEL PAINE

Grand Haven Tribune. "Attempt at Murder Near Nunica." Tuesday, December 2, 1913.
———. "Case Still a Mystery." Saturday, December 6, 1913.
———. "George Clippert Interurban Dispatcher Under Arrest." Wednesday, December 3, 1913.

———. "George Clippert Released." Thursday, December 4, 1913.
———. "Hazel Paine Case Baffles All." Friday, December 5, 1913.
———. "Hazel Paine in County Jail." Wednesday, December 10, 1913.
———. "Physicians Examine Paine Girl." Thursday, December 11, 1913.
———. "Wildey's Visit Paine Girl in Jail." December 15, 1913.
Grand Rapids Press. "Clippert Is Freed in Ottawa Mystery." Thursday, December 4, 1913.
———. "Hazel Paine Is Put in Jail by Sheriff." Wednesday, December 10, 1913.
Muskegon Chronicle. "Paine Girl Closely Guarded by Relatives; All Now Silent." Friday, December 5, 1913.

THE WILSON POUND MURDER

Daily Inter Ocean. "Not Guilty." Saturday, October 30, 1875.
Grand Rapids Press. "As Death Recalls It." Saturday, July 11, 1903.
Jackson Citizen. "Deliberate Butchery." Tuesday, July 6, 1875.
———. "The Examination of John H & Melvin Fuller." Saturday, July 17, 1875.
———. "Found Guilty." Tuesday, November 2, 1875.
———. "The Pound Murders." Tuesday, August 17, 1875.
———. "Put Over One Term." Thursday, August 12, 1875.

BANK ROBBERS AND MOBSTERS

Beck, Katherine. "Eddie Bentz, (1894–1979) Bank Robber." History Link, August 31, 2006. http://www.historylink.org/index.cfm?DisplayPage=output.cfm&file_id=7846.
Grand Haven Tribune. "Bandit Hunt Shifts from Lake to Hudson." Saturday, August 19, 1933.
———. "Five Shot as Peoples Bank Is Held Up; Wound 1 Bandit." Friday, August 18, 1933.
Holland Evening Sentinel. "Bandits Loot Bank Here, Shoot Two, Flee." Thursday, September 29, 1932.
Seibold, David H. *Grand Haven: In the Path of Destiny.* Grand Haven, MI: D-2 Enterprises, 2008.

About the Author

Photo by Tonya Keyser.

Amberrose Hammond earned her degree in language and literature at Grand Valley State University in 2005. She is cofounder with Tom Maat of the popular website Michigan's Otherside, which showcases Michigan's strange and mysterious stories from all over the state. Her work with the website led her to develop a deep interest in fun and unusual Michigan history. Her first book published with The History Press was *Ghosts & Legends of Michigan's West Coast*.